UPROOTING

A JOURNEY TO

SHAME AND

HEALING TRAUMA AND FREEING

GUILT

THE INNER CHILD

NAOMI CARR

To my sisters: you are the most precious gifts our parents gave me. I treasure our friendships.

To my parents: thank you for the gift of life and all you've given me.

Finally, to my children and future generations: may you be free from ancestral and generational trauma.

INTRODUCTION

Life is one vast lesson. Some of us are thrust into life-altering experiences at a tender age. In embracing the lessons of my experiences and dismantling my childhood conditioning, I found my wings.

This book has been in my heart for years, but it has taken decades to bring to fruition. I'm not a therapist or psychologist, nor do I hold all the answers. However, I'm an average person who has endured life's storms, which medicines and talk therapy never alleviated, and found healing.

As a little girl, I wanted to be a mother, and as a teen, I aspired to become a youth worker to help other children like me. But, above all, the desire to help others is rooted in my soul.

In my early twenties, I became aware of my need to heal my childhood trauma and discover who I was without the oppression of my parents and the dogma of my youth. I aspired to find wholeness and set out on a healing journey that would take decades.

I endeavored to eliminate any adopted victim mentality I may have acquired because the innate wisdom we're all born with told me that wearing a cape stitched with a shiny red "V" wouldn't bring me the wholeness I sought.

The same innate wisdom told me that I'd write this book

one day, but a substantial burden rested on my shoulders: sharing my struggles constructively. I feared spreading the message that my parents were horrible and liable for the mass of shame, guilt, and disempowerment I battled. Although they played a significant role, and were at the root of it all, I am accountable for ingesting my childhood conditioning and claiming it as my truth. I also struggled with shining a negative light on my family and betraying them. I feared the repercussions and backlash from family and believers of the dogma of my youth. However, I was determined to tell my story, which requires authenticity and exposing the silence of my childhood that continues amongst family members today.

Several times my fingers stilled on the keyboard while writing my story as I anticipated these repercussions. I questioned why I was putting my life out there for all to judge. I resolved that, if my healing journey could aid others with their own, I was obligated to find the courage.

My mission in life has been to be free of fear and anxiety, to heal from trauma, and to help others. As a truth seeker, I was never satisfied with the silencing by adults in my childhood. I needed to know what life was about, which often caused discord between my parents and me.

I recall, as a little girl, aspiring to be good and do good. But who judges what is moral or immoral? This weighted question was one I considered throughout my life.

In this book, I've disclosed my trauma and conditioning while shedding light on the dogma my parents followed in raising us, and their errors. I touch on controversial subjects concerning parenting and religion throughout this book, but please know the purpose is not to offend or tear down either. Parenting is one of the most challenging jobs, and no one holds all the answers. Therefore, mistakes are bound to happen. As for religion or spirituality, I believe it is our birthright to embrace what resonates with us.

If you glean one piece of inspiration that resonates with you, I have accomplished what I intended by writing this book.

1—THE FOUNDATION

"Every day, in a hundred small ways, our children ask, 'Do you hear me? Do you see me? Do I matter?' Their behavior often reflects our response." ~ **L.R. Knost**

"It is easier to build strong children than to repair broken men." ~ **Frederick Douglass**

My first memory is from three or four years old, and it is one of terror and confusion that would become the tapestry of my childhood. I don't recall anything that took place before the moment when I was standing in my father's home office. My mother stood with me at her side, reprimanding him for the bruises on my backside.

"Look what you did to her!" Fury had echoed in her voice.

I looked around at the bruises before peering up at the towering man who was supposed to love and protect me. I trembled with fear in his presence—a fear that would define the relationship between him and me until his sudden passing in 2012.

As an adult, I wondered if it was then, or one of the subsequent times, when my mother abdicated her responsibility to protect my sisters and me. Or did she simply not know how to mother?

When I related the episode to my mother years later, she said Dad had beaten me for drinking Pepto Bismol. Of course one can understand a parent's fear upon discovering their child has ingested a substance that could hurt them, but the additional harm my father inflicted held no rhyme or reason. Often, his behavior seemed absurd, and later in life, I realized his fears, religious beliefs, and trauma guided how he raised his seven daughters.

My father was a minister and raised us in a nondenominational religion. Over the last decade or more, many have left the church and now consider it a cult. I, however, won't bother with labels because it's neither here nor there. Instead, my focus is on recounting my quest to reject my childhood conditioning and attain happiness and wholeness.

Being raised in a dogma that characterized women as objects designed by Satan, and deemed inferior to men, profoundly impacted my sense of self. The Old School mentality of my youth taught me that a woman's role in life was to be submissive to her husband, and her place was at home, in the kitchen, and her job was raising children. The teachings also discouraged women from education beyond high school and jobs outside the home. Some of these teachings were promoted by the church, and others were my father's acquired beliefs.

We were primed to fear the "world" and anything outside of our way of life. External interaction with other people not from our faith was discouraged because "if you sleep with dogs, you'll get fleas." People in the "world" were Satan's people, and if you associated with them extensively, you risked the threat of the devil claiming your soul. Seclusion was imposed upon me from the time I could talk, and it came in the form of the whole world outside of my household and church.

I suppose I've always been an observer, at least for as long as I can recall. As an inquisitive child, I used to ask lots of why-focused questions. I know how that can exhaust a parent who is stressed and trying to manage responsibilities and life. In raising my own children, I remember their endless questions of Why are the trees green? and Why do the leaves fall in the autumn? It can be mentally exhausting, but our children first discover the world through their own curiosity before the conditioned beliefs harvested from parents, teachers, peers, and society take hold. Often, we embody the biased opinions and experiences of others and profess them as our truths.

My whys (and those of an average child, I expect), consisted of "But why can't I play gym with my classmates? Why can't I attend or have sleepovers? Why can't I listen to the radio?" Inside I would scream with frustration because the constant response from my parents would be one that elicited fear. They'd recite the wrongs in wanting to attend gym class, or the danger that would befall me at another child's home or even at my grandparents', who weren't of our faith. Thus, the very foundation of my childhood was rooted in terror and suspicion of the outside world. It injected a sense of not belonging in my environment. I didn't belong in society because everyone outside of the church and my home wandered in wickedness or sought to harm me. Yet, at times, I wondered if I belonged in the family I had been born into.

I craved answers to my questions about the difference between our isolated existence and those outside. Instead, I was told "Don't question it, just believe it," and made to feel ashamed for asking such questions. Comments of "You need to have the revelation" evoked feelings of being unworthy of receiving insight. If I could be righteous, God would bless me with the revelation—a distorted perception that would overshadow my life long after I left my parents' home.

From childhood I've felt things on a grand scale, with lots of gusto and passion. My mother says, as a child, I played quietly by myself, and they rarely had to scold me. However, as I approached my teen years, awareness set in. I voiced displeasure at the injustices I saw in our household and the behaviors of those in our church. Unfortunately, my parents sought to control and silence me and labeled me rebellious, which I reveal throughout this book.

The pecking order of us girls was two older sisters with a year or so between them, then me, followed by a four-year gap between myself and the next sister, and the last three came within a year or so of each other. An example of when my emotions overtook me occurred when my father was in his room giving one of my little sisters a spanking.

As their wails echoed in the main room, I paced the floor, trying to gather the nerve to do what was in my heart. But to do so would mean defying my father's authority, which was terrifying. Finally, however, in tears, I marched to my parents' closed door and pounded on it in rising panic and shouted at my father to stop. I don't know what happened after that, or if I got in trouble, but I remember the passion within me to fight for my sister's safety.

Physical, mental, and spiritual abuse defined my childhood. I received a mixture of spankings and beatings. Many were delivered in the heat of anger and stress, and I recall how my dad's green eyes flashed with wrath and determination to control. There was no explanation or apology for their actions. Instead, they sought to break my spirit and pluck out the "rebellion." They beat you until you broke and then beat you until you quieted.

Often, they quoted the scripture line "Spare the rod and spoil the child," as though that made everything okay. They manipulated scriptures to strengthen their stance.

As an adult, my first realization that my mother was aware that the abuse was wrong came with the recollection of her warning me to steer clear of a girl in my class because her mother was a social worker. Mom was aware that if the wrong person found out about the abuse in our home, she would be in trouble. When bruises marred our arms my parents made us wear long sleeves to school, another sign they knew their actions were not acceptable by society.

I often wonder why they allowed us to attend public school, but I assume they thought the fear they had ingrained in us would ensure our silence.

From the time I was quite young, Mom gaslighted me by labeling me oversensitive—a term she declared often. She suggested that my feelings were extreme and not warranted. So I painted myself with her brush, telling myself I was flawed. I need to be stronger, I told myself. I needed to shut off my emotions because there was something wrong with how I processed events around me. So, I programmed myself with those beliefs and suppressed my feelings.

Today, my mother's perspective remains the same. When any of her children show emotions or passion, she asserts we're oversensitive. When we speak about anything beyond a superficial level, my mother squirms and almost regresses. She is uncomfortable with any display of emotion.

Many of my mother's traits and responses triggered me. With healing, and a lot of self-work, I learned not to be so reactive. Therefore, I can look at people and situations with clarity and a broader perspective, allowing me to understand the origin of their behaviors. When you approach life and its situations from a healed position, and as an observer, you'll find the critical remarks others throw at you have nothing to do with you at all. Instead, it's the individual's personal criticism of themselves projected on you.

But I'm getting ahead of myself. A lot of healing had to take place in my life, and the right tools had to be presented to me before I became the person I am today.

Early in adulthood, I learned I could be of service to those in my life by giving all of myself to them. I took on the role of problem-solver and a listening ear for all the drama, leaving me drained and feeling low. I concentrated on being a responsible and loving mother and breaking the chains of dysfunction in my family. I was a devoted wife. I gave all my time, and often my money, to help friends and family. I lived each day doing the best I knew how. Yet, I held fast to my greatest desire: that when I laid my head down at night I found solace in my treatment of others, that all who walked away from our interaction did so feeling they mattered and were heard. As saintlike as that may sound, it is the essence at my core. I gave others the voice I so desperately wanted in my life. To the best of my ability I spread respect, empathy, kindness, and compassion. Yet, never once did I consider that I owed the same to myself.

Stepping-Stone Exercises

I emphasize the importance of having a notebook to complete the assignments you will find throughout this book. However, don't devalue yourself by doing the assignments in your head. I made this error and found more success in taking the time to write out my truth.

This is the perfect time to spoil yourself with a beautiful

notebook and pen. There is healing in putting your feelings on paper.

Light a candle, and if you're a lover of coffee like me, brew yourself a cup and cozy up on the couch or armchair with your favorite throw. Or if it's a warm, sunny day, nourish yourself with a glass of water, and sit outside and bask in the rays. Gift yourself with the time you deserve to begin your healing journey.

Inside the notebook's cover write your name, and then run your fingers over the handwriting. Take a moment to appreciate that there is only one of you, and that our world needs you. Then, say aloud or in your mind, "I honor myself by putting myself first. I deserve to be free and happy."

The first step in freeing yourself from guilt and shame, and healing from trauma, is acknowledging the truth of your past. Not your parents' or siblings' truth, but yours.

How you start to heal the trauma takes work, but you are worth the effort. You have the power to heal yourself.

My goal with this book and the assignments is to share the tools that worked for me in hopes you will find your own freedom.

To heal, we must acknowledge the pain and set it free.

Let's start with your first memory. Write it down. What feelings surfaced with that memory? Were the feelings joyous, fearful, or sad? Allow your emotions to flow as fluidly as your ink.

As we work through the chapters and written exercises, there will be days when you feel drained because revisiting the pain is hard, but I promise you it will subside, and in time, the growth that comes with healing will transcend the ache.

Remember, it is your time to shine. You matter, and you are worth the work.

2–INGRAINED

"A child must know that he is a miracle, that since the beginning of the world there hasn't been, and until the end of the world there will not be, another child like him." ~
Pablo Casals

Pressed against my father's side in the armchair, I clutched my reader, *Fun with Dick and Jane*, in trembling hands. Panic churned my tummy and squeezed my throat as I stumbled over the words, willing them to come out correctly. I kept my father's assurance, displayed across the arm of the worn armchair, in my peripheral vision. The gleaming zipper stretched from one end to the other of the black leather belt, and memories of the sting and snakelike imprint it'd leave in my flesh evoked terror. (Such occurrences continued into and throughout my adolescence.)

My parents' decision to enroll us in a Mennonite homeschooling program in grade five amplified my struggle to learn. Homeschool in those days wasn't what it is today, and with so many kids for my mother to teach, some of us fell between the cracks and failed to receive an education for two or more years before we were returned to the public school system—me in my eighth year, junior high.

As an adult, I struggle to read with precision and clarity because I'd learned to rush and skip words in my hurry to be done and remove myself from harm's way. It permeated me with embarrassment, and shame and stripped me of confidence. As a result, I spent years feeling stupid and uneducated, despite being an educated, successful entrepreneur.

Although I prided myself in being an authentic person, I often felt like a fraud. I displayed confidence like a faux fur coat. Before entering a room, I'd take a deep breath, square my shoulders, jut out my chin, put on a fetching smile, and march into the room. Despite the pins and needles coursing through my body, and how I quivered inside, I'd resolved to never let anyone detect my vulnerability. Never again would I become the helpless little girl of my youth. I was determined to be in control of myself and what happened to me. I'd become an expert at wrapping myself in a false sense of security.

My lack of confidence caused me to second-guess my word choices when speaking, and I often jumbled words together to get them out. When people gave me their full attention, I'd retreat from the spotlight because I worried that people would consider me uneducated and inferior. This, along with my struggles to read aloud, evoked anxiety at speaking in front of a room full of people. So I dimmed my light to guarantee I never did. I felt powerless and loathed myself for what I considered a weakness. I desperately wanted to be the confident and charismatic woman I portrayed.

During a business trip some years ago, I sat at a boardroom table surrounded by women. By this point in my life, I'd built my confidence and established a mindset to uproot the need to stay hidden from the world. I'd embraced my talents and had begun to share my gifts.

As the meeting progressed I observed the other women, who eyed me with interest. True to my usual composure, I presented an outer appearance of poise as I listened attentively to the speaker. Nevertheless, as the heat of the women's gazes lingered, my throat constricted and nausea stirred. Ignoring their stares, I silently prayed that I'd avoid the discussion and attempted to make myself small, which at five foot seven was impossible. Not to mention, the previous day, we'd been asked to reveal a little about ourselves and our accomplishments, and in doing so, I'd fueled the intrigue of the others. Desperate to deflect their attention, I placed my undivided attention on the speaker. To my dismay, she turned to me and said, "I'd love to hear from Naomi."

All eyes in the room registered on me. Panic snatched my breath. Good god, no! Please no! My stomach lurched, and my flesh zapped as the room faded around me and their faces melded into the blur. I disconnected from my body in a full-blown fight-or-flight response. Yet I sensed the quiet blanketing the room, and I grappled to gain control before I humiliated myself.

The faces in the room took form, and I observed how their eyes regarded me with eagerness and anticipation. I took a deep breath and thought, *Well, here goes nothing. My cover is blown. As soon as I start talking and jumbling my words, they'll know I'm a fraud.*

I talked for only a few minutes, but I spoke from a place of authenticity and passion about what I'd learned in my profession. When I concluded, and the meeting had ended, I slipped from the boardroom as quickly as possible and returned to the safety of my hotel room, where I scrutinized everything I'd said, and how I'd said it. *You should have said this*, I reprimanded myself as feelings of shame and embarrassment rose. Dammit. Why hadn't I declined? I would've been better off. Now I had to face them tomorrow, and for the rest of the week. *You probably sounded like a blabbering fool.* I went to bed berating myself, but rose the next day and summoned the courage to walk to the breakfast room.

I'd become highly skilled in managing day-to-day interactions despite debilitating anxiety and an uncertainty of my environment. I forced myself to show up in life and not hide in the corner despite wanting to do precisely that.

I strode into the room with a fixed smile and glowed with self-assurance. I could've sat alone to avoid the pending inquiries and in an attempt to shield myself from humiliation. But I refused to be isolated and avoided the effects of seclusion at all costs. I injected myself into society as a functioning person, despite wanting to jump out of my skin during encounters where I felt out of control.

I seated myself across from another woman who had been at the meeting the previous night and hurried to steer the conversation to light small talk, smiling and laughing while wondering what she thought of me. As our table filled with the other women my nerves thrummed, and the walls around me felt like they were caving in. I waited for them to interrogate me and to pick apart my speech.

A lady positioned herself across from me and leaned in, regarding me with admiration. She said, "I really enjoyed your input last night. It was inspiring and educational. It gives me hope that I can find the same success."

I gulped, dumbfounded at her comment, but quickly collected myself and smiled at her. "Aww, thank you," I said sincerely.

I absorbed her compliment and dislodged the initial uneasiness at her praise. Others chimed in to agree with her, and my cheeks heated at the attention. However, the barbed wire that had draped my flesh like a shield of protection as they sat down parted with the realization that they sought to empower and posed no threat. I evaluated the mass of undue stress and anxiety I'd caused myself, and how my projected inner criticism had been the culprit.

Self-doubt had become a finely tuned merry-go-round governing my life. My mistrust in myself and others, along with my lack of self-esteem, felt suffocating. So I aimed to disarm it, recognizing most of my issues stemmed from childhood; and if I hoped to attain peace, I had to clean up any residue adhering beneath the surface. Yet, despite spending years working on myself, no matter what I'd tried, I couldn't get free.

In my attempts, I evaluated my triggers and reactions to a situation. I realized I placed emphasis on what others thought of me, often viewing myself through their eyes, as I had at breakfast with my colleagues. The "attagirl" they had given me elicited the joy of being seen and appreciated for simply being me.

In revisiting the emotions I experienced with those ladies, I also reflected on my childhood and the lack of praise. Instead of building me up and instilling confidence, my parents tore me down by focusing on their concepts of right and wrong, which were dictated by their unhealed selves and the dogma they followed. Recognition of good had been withheld. If given, it came immersed in the toxicity of my childhood.

Too often, we measure ourselves through others' eyes, gleaning a sense of satisfaction for only a fleeting moment because outside approval never lasts. When we learn to accept ourselves and stop craving outside approval, we achieve true happiness and peace.

To expand on my experience during that breakfast, another woman sat down across from me to my left. I'd already placed her in one of the various categories I assigned people. The previous day, I had formed an opinion of her from her display of intrusive and self-serving behavior. However, as she seated herself, she also offered me praise, but internally I rejected her opinion. Again I unfurled my barbed wire shield, granting her a fixed smile and politeness while leaving her on the "proceed with caution" shelf and regarding her with inward leeriness.

To my astonishment, she offered me a paid position on a board, helping others in our profession, but I retreated. Nope, that wasn't for me, I told myself. I liked being my own boss and didn't want anyone overseeing me. Although true, it wasn't why I never considered her offer. I couldn't possibly do such a thing, I said to myself. Part of me was elated at the thought of motivating others. But how could I educate and encourage others when speaking in front of a group made my stomach twist into knots? I quickly declined the position and said I was too busy. Again valid, but not the reason behind my rejection of the job.

Later that day, at lunch with some of the women, one opened up about her fear of reading in front of others, and I piped up and said, "Me too." The person who had offered me the paid position looked at me, eyes narrowed, as the other woman went on to explain she had dyslexia. I wished I could retract my words because I didn't believe I had dyslexia and felt I'd spoken too soon.

"So, that's why you don't want to do it?"

I gulped back the nerves constricting my throat and regarded the woman who had made me the offer. "I'm willing to help others by speaking one-on-one, but not in front of a room of people. I also don't like to read in front of others because I stumble over my words."

Again, her brow puckered, and feeling stuck with no way out, I decided to let down my guard and reveal my vulnerability.

I shared a brief insight into my background and how I was a work in progress. Then the dreaded pity flickered in their eyes, and I retreated. I didn't want anyone's pity. I didn't want to be a weirdo on the playground that kids avoided, like they had in my youth. Hence I calmed the yearning to fit into a world I'd been trained to believe I didn't and suppressed my quiver of emotions.

As the conversation turned to other subjects, I questioned if I had played the victim role by sharing. I'd become hypersensitive to donning a victim mentality because I'd witnessed too many succumb to their past woes and become stuck. Early in my adult life, I decided that although I'd lost my right to be a child, I wouldn't let it rob me of my future. Therefore I strove for success in all aspects of my life, often becoming an overachiever. Despite the mindset I'd formed to not allow my upbringing to hold me back, it did, and in ways that took decades to dispel.

Early on in adulthood I tried to talk to my mother about my childhood and the pain and fear I carried, but she wasn't a safe place to reveal my vulnerability. The opposite, in fact. Her denial of the sufferings at their hands became suffocating, and my turning to her was harmful. Her denial messed with my head and made me question my memories, and at times, I wondered if I had made it all up. The mental battle of sorting through the truth, Mom's fallacies, and my sisters' unwillingness to deal with the past filled me with frustration and confusion.

No one enjoys dealing with heartache and pain, but to heal I had to face the harm done to my psyche. So, many days, I didn't want to show up in life. I longed to pull the covers over my head and forget the world existed. I wanted to cancel my therapy appointments. I dreaded therapy and talking about my childhood because it made me feel horrible. I left the therapist's office feeling like I'd been the rope in a tug-of-war between ferocious dogs.

The patterns of intimidation and fear throughout my childhood reveal my parents were unhealed. The aggressive way my father handled his children was behavior I witnessed in his siblings and their handling of my cousins. Thus, the generational trauma in my family is extensive. I've made it my mission to do my part to stop the cycle and heal myself. In my self-discovery process, I realized that I've never been a big reader outside of blogs and research to better understand subjects I'm passionate about. I only truly enjoy a fiction book when I'm on vacation and in a place of complete relaxation. However, I have collected many nonfiction books and practice reading aloud. As a result, I've formed a newfound appreciation for reading, which goes to show we're never too old to relearn and take our power back.

I'm a work in progress, and I've become okay with that.

Stepping-Stone Exercises

Take the time to settle into a safe space you've created where you won't be disturbed.

First, place a hand on your heart, and allow your face to soften as you thank yourself for showing up today. By simply showing up, you took another step toward claiming the future you deserve. Well done!

Awareness of my emotions and reactions to situations required me to assess why I experienced them. When we are unhealed, we are reactive and triggered. To be free of triggers, we must first understand where they originate.

Let's start with your insecurities. We've all experienced them. Write down your top two. Now, consider times when these vulnerabilities and self-doubts have caused you to lash out or retreat. Is there a memory that pops up? If so, evaluate what emotions or pain is attached to the memory.

With a candid evaluation of ourselves, we bring clarity

and recognize ourselves in a new light. It is in these private and honest reflections that we can get to the source of our conditioning.

For example, you've carried the belief that you are unintelligent. Did someone insert this belief in you? And, when in your life did you adapt to their opinion and make it your truth?

Take the judge's seat. Your observations are on trial. As the only judge of your life, you hold the final say. Do their claims hold any weight?

Write three things that prove their statement invalid. Now write three things to extract their input that you've allowed to influence your life too much.

Example: I am intelligent. I am brilliant. I approve of me.

You may not believe these affirmations right now. But adding positive affirmations to your daily life uproots old, programmed beliefs. It will change your internal monologue to one that will uplift and change your life.

When affirmations were introduced to me, I laughed. As if something so simple could help. But it did! My life is a testament to how they help. Now I smile at how simple tools are precisely what I needed to guide me along my journey to wholeness. They were the stepping- stones to standing bold and proud in the life I continue to show up to each day, with joy and eagerness.

For the rest of the day, while making dinner or going for a walk, repeat these affirmations. Perhaps each time you go to the restroom and pause to wash your hands, look in the mirror and repeat to the beautiful soul peering back at you the positive affirmations you wrote. The person in the mirror is your greatest ally, but have you made them your enemy?

3—THE PREY

"Fears are educated into us, and can, if we wish,
be educated out." ~ **Karl Augustus Menninger**

Although I sought to be rid of my past, it pursued me like a shadow, causing me to manage life with an iron grip. The urgent need to control who entered my circle and my environment was ever-present. As a result, life became a balancing act between deep contemplation and sorting through continual self-doubt. Without the influence of healthy adults to rely on, I tuned into my intuition and heart, and they became my compass.

For years, I couldn't speak of my past without bursting into tears. The times when I let my walls down long enough to share my truth with a friend or a therapist, I'd break down, then feel embarrassed about my vulnerability. Afterward, I'd run the conversation on repeat in my head, second-guessing myself that I said too much. What if they reported my parents? My family would disown me. Was I betraying my parents? Shame ran untamed within me. Maybe I was making too much of what had happened. Had I deluded myself and exaggerated the truth? The vicious cycle of guilt and shame governed my life.

In the first years of therapy, I was selective with what I

shared, and when we dug too deep, I bailed and wouldn't go back for several years. Treatment brought up all the pain but never seemed to allay it.

I learned to repress my memories, attempting to make myself believe it wasn't as bad as I remembered. I'd say things like, "At least I wasn't raised in a house where I was molested, or where my parents were alcoholics, because that would be far worse."

But then I'd recall how Dad loved to see us girls run in fear, like it was a sick, twisted urge inside him—a grin would split his face, and his eyes twinkled at the very sight.

Even now, it pains my heart to know he found pleasure in these so-called games. Mom's explanation and dismissal of his behavior was that Dad loved to tease and torment, which he did, but it's not an excuse for his behavior. Other times, she'd claim, "I can't believe that happened. I would've stopped it." Yet memories of daughters seeking protection behind her skirt hold weight.

Today, her denial continues to be her shield, and she portrays Dad as her savior, claiming that if he was alive, he'd save his daughters from our sins. She feels grave disappointment in her children and states it when we do not yield to her demands.

In her refusal to acknowledge the abuse, she stirred the cauldron of pain and anger simmering in the pit of my belly. Interactions with her silently charged me with disgust for the woman who bore me. A pro at stifling my pain and emotions, I conformed to the teachings of my rearing. She was my elder, so I remained silent, giving away my power.

For decades, the memories of the house of horrors permeated my dreams, and I'd wake sobbing and shaken.

One "game" my father found thrilling haunted me for years. He'd line us up from oldest to youngest in front of the kitchen cupboards, ensuring there was space between each of us. Then, belt in hand, he'd stand back and say he was doing it to guarantee we never misbehaved. A murmur of weeping would ripple through the line, and I remember how my whole body shook with terror. I recall how my sisters' faces mirrored my own panic and how I ached to reach out and comfort them, but fear kept me rooted. I squeezed my eyes shut, waiting for the blow. The first strike would land on the sister of his choosing, and as her wail reverberated, it snatched my breath.

For the fun of it, he delivered a calculated blow at the space between us, and the cupboard echoed the impact, which was his way of demonstrating how much it'd hurt when your turn came. But, unfortunately, he never went in order, so you never knew when your turn was coming. Therefore, there was no time to squeeze your butt tight in hopes of alleviating some of the pain.

Another of his "games" was to chase us through the house with the belt, snapping it to remind us he pursued us, and like a hound chasing rabbits set free in a maze, our predator barked at our heels. We were brainwashed into believing these games were okay.

For years, the sight of a belt would make my knees go weak. Then, in the early years of our marriage, my husband would fold his belt and snap it to make a loud noise before getting dressed. Despite my request that he refrain from doing so, he never stopped.

One day, as he dressed, I sat on our bed talking to him, and he grabbed his belt to put it on, but first, he folded it and did a quick snap. Triggered, my body tensed, and I asked him to stop, panic rising inside me. Instead he did it again. I crumpled into a fetal position and wept as the terror of the games from my childhood returned.

Astonished at my distress, he dropped the belt and raced to

me and gathered me in his arms, sympathy in his eyes. At that moment, he realized how deeply his actions had impacted me. We discussed how it shouldn't have come to that point for him to hear me. After that, he never fooled around with the belt again.

My father's dominating personality, along with the stance of the men of the church and their power over women, significantly shaped my anxiety around men and authority figures. I braced like a warrior ready for battle when they neared, especially men in uniform and authoritative positions.

I often questioned how I ended up married, with my leeriness toward the opposite sex. But, in all honesty, I doubted I would have if I hadn't met my husband. We were high school sweethearts and married at eighteen and twenty. I often tease that, because I'm the older one, I should be the boss. We were so young to take on marriage, but we established a bond early on. We were raised in the same dogma, and we'd both experienced dysfunctional childhoods. His gentle manner, kindness, and compassion helped me lower my guard enough to let him get close. He's been my rock and has taught me the true meaning of love, and I haven't always made it easy for him. He says the same about himself.

Despite him doing nothing to deserve it, I feared earning his disapproval. So, regardless of how tidy I kept our home, some days, when I had a tough day or was too busy with the kids and work to have the house in order, I'd panic when he walked in the door, fearing the phantom of his wrath.

As children, when Dad drove into the yard, we jumped and scrambled around the house, looking for anything to clean or fix to avoid punishment. Before leaving to go to town or run errands, he would order us to find certain objects, claiming to have barrels and barrels of them, and if we hadn't located them by the time he returned, we would be punished. So we searched high and low for the items, all the while fearing what would happen if we didn't find them. I believe he wanted us to fear him and took pleasure in our terror.

As children of abuse, we often allow others to fill the former position of our abusers upon reaching adulthood. For example, we get involved in relationships with abusive partners or become addicted to drugs, sex, alcohol, gambling, shopping, or food. All with the desire to numb the pain and fill the void. It's an emptiness that can never be satisfied from outside sources.

We hold the key to unlock the cage and free ourselves from our predators. The choice is ours. We can remain captive to our past, or show up as a participant in our daily lives and be the creator of our future. In healing our wounds, we discover our worth and true happiness.

4 – GROOMED

"Trauma fractures comprehension as a pebble shatters
a windshield. The wound at the site of impact spreads
across the field of vision, obscuring reality and
challenging belief." ~ **Jane Leavy**

One day, when I was around eight or ten, friends of my
parents were visiting, and I recall standing next to my
father while he and his friend sat at the table, chatting.
An interaction—what my young mind had considered play—
occurred between my father and I. I don't recollect how it began,
but I recall him smiling, and I laughed and swatted back at him.
Then the smile slipped from his face, and his green eyes flashed.
I knew I'd done something gravely wrong. He leaped to his feet
and hauled me into the nearby bathroom and closed the door
before proceeding to strike me across the face, again and again,
until my bladder released.

"I've got to pee," I wailed between blows.

He allowed me to use the toilet before hitting me another
time or two. After he left, I stood numb and bewildered and an-
alyzed what I had done wrong. I had to have hurt him. I shoul-
dered the blame.

Reflecting on the incident, I wondered why the friend never

intervened. He would have heard what was happening. If they spoke to my parents in private, nothing changed.

For the longest time, the silence from spectators puzzled me. If teachers suspected everything wasn't okay at home, they never reported it. I assume it had a lot to do with the silencing of many injustices in that era.

I remember my maternal grandfather, a gentle soul whom I adored, tried a time or two to step in, but to no avail. He lived five miles or so from us, and when he came to visit, he always had hard candy and would give us each a piece. He had the most fantastic head of silver hair, and his laughter was infectious. Despite the deep sorrows and losses life had dealt him, he showered love and kindness in the world and touched the hearts and lives of many.

My fondest memory of him was when he would come by our house and take us girls and his youngest daughter, Katie, for rides in the back of his truck. In those days it was legal, and I smile as I think of the eight of us crammed into the bed of his little blue pickup. He would drive the back dirt roads with his window down and his arm resting on the door ledge. Us girls giggled and hooted with glee, delighting in our freedom. I recall peering at him through the back window of the cab and noting the beautiful smile on his face as he basked in our joy.

I look back at him with fondness, and am so grateful for the love he showed us. I'm honored to have called him my grandfather.

My step-grandmother had a brash nature but showed her love in her own way. My mother had personal issues with her stepmother and wouldn't let us call her grandmother, so we referred to her by her first name. I assume my mother's loyalty to her deceased mother is where it originated. Regardless of the relationship between her and my mother, she embraced her husband's grandchildren and never made us feel separate from her other grandkids. She made sure that we got gifts at Christmas, and we looked forward to them. My step-grandmother didn't offer praise often. I recall spending the night at her house while my mother gave birth to one of my sisters in the hospital. I brought her a spelling test to sign. I was beaming with pride because I'd received an A+ and was confident she would be proud of me. I stood back while she regarded my test and waited with anticipation, but instead of receiving the "attagirl" I sought, she looked at me, and with a click of her tongue, said, "With handwriting like that, I would never have given you an A+." Her words crushed my spirit.

Regardless of her gruff personality and how it made me timid around her, I have many fond memories of her, and like my grandfather, she holds a special place in my heart. She used to take us berry-picking for wild strawberries and would openly talk to us about life. I felt safe in her company. I am grateful for her efforts to bond with us, regardless of her and my mother not seeing eye to eye.

My grandparents were not wealthy, and my step-grandmother had a large family from her deceased husband, three adopted kids, and many grandchildren. Nevertheless, she purchased daughters' pride rings for each of us, and when I was graduating, she insisted I have a grad ring. I know she fought to ensure I got the grad ring because my parents were going through a phase where jewelry and barrettes were sinful. Her efforts made me feel she believed in me and saw me as valuable to the world.

In my tenth year of high school, I had to stay after school, then walked to my grandparents' house to wait for my parents to pick me up. Katie, my grandfather's daughter with my step-grandmother, was a year younger than me, and we formed a bond that was never severed. She wanted me to stay longer and hang with her. I figured the answer would be no because my parents limited our interaction with others outside our faith and household. I gathered the courage to call and ask. My dad answered the phone, and upon my request, he became angry and belittled me for asking. I hung up the phone and returned to her room, where she was hanging out with two other girls from school. I informed them I couldn't stay. Overwhelmed by my father's behavior and fear of his wrath when he arrived to pick me up, I started to cry.

Perhaps my grandfather overheard my conversation with my father because he came to the room and told me to go to the kitchen, that he and my step-grandmother wanted to speak to me. They sat me down and said that I could live with them if I ever needed a place to stay. I gulped at the seriousness in their faces, realizing that they saw and disagreed with what was happening at home. As an adult, I appreciate and recognize the courage it took for them to be willing to defy my dad, who was an intimidating presence to most.

Groomed to fear the various "worldly" people who came in and out of my grandparents' house, anxiety over the hurt they'd inflict on me outweighed what could possibly happen at home. At least there, I knew what to expect. "Worldly" people were capable of far worse, so I declined their offer and never told my parents.

My father's family rarely came to visit, although they lived half an hour away. Mom claimed her fear of us doing something wrong and upsetting our grandmother was why these relationships were never nurtured. The drama between my father, his parents, and his siblings was a strong narrative in my childhood. After he became their pastor, the chasm in the family only increased.

The isolation from the outside world became unbearable. I struggled to feel connected to my body far into my adult years. I experienced my first full-blown panic attack when I was around twenty-four years old and grappled with them until my midthirties. I spent most of my life looking over my shoulder and around every corner, waiting for the attack I'd been groomed to believe would come. My skin crawled with tension. I felt like a wind-up alarm clock. *Tick. Tick. Tick.* I waited for the alarm to sound and for hell to be unleashed.

5—THE HEALING FREEDOM OF LAUGHTER

"Your body cannot heal without play. Your mind cannot heal without laughter. Your soul cannot heal without joy." ~
Catherine Rippenger Fenwick

Late one evening, after the rest of the house fell quiet, I sat in the kitchen of our old farmhouse while my mother stood at the sink washing dishes.

Perhaps from exhaustion, or for some other reason, I took to giggling, which turned into laughter.

Mom whirled around and scowled at me, and said, "Stop it right now, Naomi. Jesus doesn't like foolishness."

I quickly sobered, and as she returned to her task, I frowned at her safely turned back. Confusion seized my young mind. God doesn't like laughter. Did He not have a sense of humor or joy in his heart?

The God of my youth was to be feared. He was out there somewhere, watching and judging my every move. When judgment day came and I wasn't ready, I would surely burn in the pits of hell. Or one day I'd awake, and my family would have been taken to heaven in the rapture, and I'd be left to wander the earth, where suffering and torture was rampant. For decades I had nightmares of searching for my family and not finding them because I had been unworthy of making it to heaven. I learned that earning God's love took a lot of effort, and because I wasn't granted the revelation of the preordained people, the "one" group that would make it to heaven, the terror of the end of days dominated my life until the age of twenty-eight.

Not only was my childhood immersed in abuse, fear, anxiety, and trauma, which is a chore to heal from, but connected with the brainwashing of my parents' dogma, it ignites feelings of being injured and stranded on a cliff with no way down.

After I left home and started my own life, which I will relate later in this book, the silence of my parents' disappointment and shame plagued me. They regarded me as an outsider and part of the "world." They restricted my younger sisters from communicating with me, and the hurt burrowed deep inside me. My parents prayed for me to be saved and consistently reminded me of my need to get right with God. My mother went so far as to use my children by reminding me what would happen to them in hell if my husband and I didn't turn back to their faith. Their dogma taught that children are covered under the parents' faith until they're of age to be saved, which means giving their heart to God and being baptized. Shame, terror, and guilt kept me awake at night. Why was I so bent on being free of my childhood, and the doctrine, that I would willingly sacrifice my children to a life of damnation? I was unfit to be a parent. My kids deserved better. The battle inside me was brutal. Considered unsaved by them, I calculated my worth through their eyes.

Many of my sisters supported the teachings of our youth until recently, which caused a rift. Their steadfast belief and my refusal to be guided by fear into believing something I didn't fracture our bond. Although my love for my sisters never dwindled, I found it hard to connect on an authentic level with them. Seeking to protect myself from more hurt, I held them at arm's length. My sisters and I talk often, but I still sense the gap between us. I respect their choice for those who continue to follow the faith, as I believe it's our birthright to support what resonates with us.

However, it comes with challenges because relationships with people who don't appreciate what you say unless it aligns with their views are complex. Healthy communication is like a hose with the faucet turned on. There's a natural flow of energy and positive exchange. However, with the mentality of people in my family's faith, there's a kink in the hose. And because I wear pants and cut my hair, everything out of my mouth is taken at face value. I witness the shift in their eyes as their ears close to my opinions. No wisdom I may carry holds any importance to them because I'm less than in their eyes. As a result, I often felt rejected and devalued, and the pain of their dismissal pursued me for years.

To further explain how their doctrine works, if I were to sit at a table of these "believers" and a man was present, he'd be asked to share the blessing over the food because a woman being too verbose is frowned upon. On the other hand, if I were with a group of women "believers," I also wouldn't be asked to say the blessing. Their tenet is that God doesn't hear the prayers of women who cut their hair; therefore the food wouldn't be blessed.

I hold little merit in the company of so-called family members regardless of my morals and values because they consider me a sinner. It's challenging to feel like you belong in a family with extreme dynamics like this. It makes it equally hard for me, my husband, and my children because my husband's family also follows the doctrine.

My mother wasn't raised in the dogma of my father's family. When she met my father, he'd left the religion and would be considered a partyer, but after a few years of marriage, he returned to the faith, and Mom joined him. He followed the dogma until his death, and my mother stands firm in the teachings today. For other reasons concerning her behavior, and her need to condemn others for not believing her faith, I've had to put firm boundaries in place to have any manner of relationship with her.

The dominating approach my parents used when it came to their doctrine puzzled me. You couldn't think for yourself, and if you did, it was all wrong. They inserted their own timing in how they thought your relationship with God should unfold. For example, when I was around seventeen years old, my father made me kneel at my bedside and insisted I pray aloud. Then, belt in hand, he positioned himself on my sister's bed across from me to wait. Of course I obeyed, and meekly forced out the words.

"Louder," he said, and struck me with the belt.

Terrified, I obliged, and the insincere prayer fell from my lips. He hit me another time or two, until my pitch was to his liking.

The same forceful treatment applied to my baptism. It never came from my desire, but more because I was thirteen, and what would people think? My parents gave too much leverage to what others thought. Nevertheless, I followed through with the baptism because what choice did I have? Afterward, in the churchyard, my mother said something to me, and I said something back. My dad overheard and proceeded to disparage me, stating I had just been baptized yet I behaved like my former self. In my head, I said words I'd never dare breathe aloud for fear it would be the last words I spoke: "I never wanted to get baptized. That was your doing." I regarded him, making sure to keep my emotions in check, while inside, I felt like a failure and a disappointment.

From when I was a preteen until I left home, my older sisters and I shouldered the responsibility of my younger siblings. These responsibilities included bathing, homework, preparing food, and caring for and comforting them when they were sick. The list goes on. The "little girls," as we still refer to them today, had several mothers in their lives. Although Mom was alive and present, she reassigned her duty as a mother to us older girls.

Great responsibility was something I was used to, and my second job was as a nanny on the army base. No wonder why—I excelled at being a mother figure. The two children in my care clung to me and often cried for me when I went out, instead of their own mother, who, like my mother, was also present but self-serving. Her happiness took precedence over her children. I bonded with those children, and I grieved the loss when I moved on.

When I became a mother at twenty-one, parenting came naturally to me. I easily fit the role of mother and wife, and managed a household like a pro. My children's physical and emotional needs were met. My bills and rent were paid on time. We didn't have a lot of money in those days, so when it was payday and I had to buy groceries, I sat down with a list of what I needed and placed an amount beside the item: milk $4, butter $2, diapers $25. I prided myself on how I'd stay within a couple dollars of the amount I'd budgeted.

As life went on around me, I never stepped out of form. I had a duty to my husband and my children, and often, as we parents do, I never put myself into the equation. Consideration for myself wasn't part of my conditioning. Fun wasn't part of my makeup, or so I believed.

We've been conditioned to believe putting ourselves first is selfish. However, as mental health awareness has taken a more critical position in the past few decades, research reveals the benefits of taking care of ourselves first. In becoming present in your life as a healthy, healed individual, those around you reap the blessings.

The vast depths of my conditioning, and the list of rights and wrongs, took years to uproot. Playing golf was wrong. Going to the movies, also wrong. Wearing makeup or piercing your ears, also bad. Dating required chaperones and took place during the daylight hours because, after dark, the devil came out, making young people act in sinful ways. Holding hands, kissing, or having sex before marriage was forbidden. I was married two years before I stopped feeling dirty for having sex with my husband. As a couple raised in the same faith and taught to suppress sexuality and pleasure responses, you can imagine the struggles that came with seeking to have a healthy sex life. As difficult as it has been, I can't imagine how it would've worked out if we'd chosen different partners who couldn't relate to why we repressed this part of us. I opposed my body and myself. Daily, I denounced myself with a negative internal dialogue. Like the lash applied to my own back, I condemned all my self-acclaimed mistakes and shortcomings. Berating myself was mentally exhausting. I never allowed myself grace.

The intensity of my conditioning molded me into a rigid person. I never liked to look foolish. I looked like the average person on the outside, but inside, I was the young girl drowning in dogma, fear, and confusion. Internally, I was too serious. Yet on the outside, I behaved like a carefree spirit. I smiled, offered respect, kindness, empowerment, and compassion to all. I was an expert at taking control of a conversation and making it lighthearted. In friendships and interactions with others, I craved laughter and positive energy. Unfortunately, although I yearned for positive-minded friends, I drew the opposite. The women I befriended often came with a lot of baggage and negativity. I subjected myself to their belittling of me to make themselves feel better. In their own need to take command of their surroundings, they'd seek to manage me and others I built friendships with. For a time, because I didn't consider my worth and had been so used to having no say in my decisions, I allowed others to control me. Often, I disagreed with their views but would let them believe I agreed because fear of rejection ran rampant in me.

Early friendships dealt me some hard knocks, and the hardships from one in particular hurled me over the edge into anxiety and anguish. I experienced my first panic attack, and they would terrorize me for a decade.

The desperation to win back the friendship ended at her hand would claim six years of my life. Throughout those years, when I thought of her, I'd sometimes send flowers, email a song that made me think of her, or send an email relating how much I cared before proceeding to take the blame for something I never did. I couldn't understand her paranoia or rationale, and I strived to fix something she wasn't mentally capable or willing to work on. The severity of the gaslighting I endured during those six years did take its toll on me. The absurd amount of energy I wasted to try mending the relationship caused me significant stress and hurt. The absurd thing was, I was aware of how drained I felt for a week after dealing with her before the friendship even ended, and after. It wasn't the friendship I strove to reclaim but the restoration of peace in my life. Finally, I came to my senses and stopped tormenting myself by attempting to repair something that wasn't healthy for me. I let go and never looked back.

Despite walking away, I carried the baggage of the friendship with me. For years, anger at this person simmered inside me. I blamed her for the panic attacks and for stealing my power. My self-worth only diminished after that experience. It was after this that I began to question my sanity and everything about myself. Already dealing with relentless anxiety, I felt like I'd lose my bloody mind most days. I began to evaluate every interaction I had and grew leery of forming new friendships. I spent too much time considering my behavior and conversations with friends and what it would cost me if I said the wrong thing. This behavior continued for a couple of years. I'd leave time spent with a friend to later call them or tell them the next time we saw each other that I was sorry for this and that, and I hadn't meant to hurt them if anything I'd said did. They'd look at me as though I was crazy, and at their reaction, I'd cringe in shame. Again, I began the process of berating myself. What is wrong with you? You're acting like a bloody fool. You aren't normal. What must they think of you? It was a vicious cycle.

Ugh, I'm exhausted remembering those days. I want to reach into the past, hug my former self, and tell her it will be okay. And remind her, you've got this, girl! How much better would tenderness and self-love have served me?

In time, I realized the loss of the relationship all those years ago, the struggles and the heartbreak I endured, had given me a backbone. It molded me into a different person. It drove me to value myself and not let others manipulate or control me. Too often, we think that things are done "to" us when they are actually done "for" us. It's in the experiences that we learn the lessons.

With the friendships that followed, I had developed a kernel of self-confidence, and when it was time for a relationship to end, I allowed it to naturally dwindle. In my late twenties, I started hanging out with a group of women who insisted on hugging each other goodbye each time we parted at the gym or on lunch and coffee dates. I complied to avoid discrimination or appearing too uptight, but I braced upon contact. Loving and safe physical touch hadn't been part of my childhood, and again, if it was, it had been swallowed up by toxicity. As Mark Wolynn states in his book, *It Didn't Start with You*, there's a reason for this. He says, "Where we, as small children, experienced our safety or security being threatened, our bodies reacted by erecting defenses. These unconscious defenses then become our default, orienting our attention toward what's difficult or unsettling, instead of registering what's comforting."

I continued to draw friends that required a lot of work. After hanging out with them, more times than not, I'd return home exhausted and feeling low because the conversations were weighed down in gossip and negativity. I never allowed people to get too close, and as long as the focus wasn't on my faults, I learned to swallow how awful I felt after leaving. Guilt plagued me because gossiping never felt good to me. It didn't matter if we shared the good or the bad happening to people. I believe people's business should be exactly that—their business.

When we succumb to gossip and criticism of others, we need to stop and reflect on what we are feeling. You will find it has nothing to do with them, and everything to do with our inner critic; our own shame, guilt, anger, and absence of self-love. Discussing people's affairs or criticizing others won't make you feel better, or ease the ache and emptiness inside. Such conversations only saddled me with more shame because, as my gut warned me, "It's not them. It's you."

I felt like a captive in my mind and body. I hauled around suitcases of shame, guilt, and self-loathing. Despite having created a beautiful life with a great man, and my two beautiful children, I felt empty and on edge. I lived in the world in isolation, which is no way to live. The fortress I built around my heart to ward off people left me seeking security in a world that felt foreign to me. Unfortunately, although I was self-aware of my need to heal, I was far from being whole. Therapy only rehashed the past and left me hanging on a limb, waiting for the branch to snap. Moreover, it never provided the tools required to heal.

I continued to make friendships that never gave anything to me in return. I'm referring to the positive exchange of energy I mentioned earlier. After hanging out with my girlfriends, I would often walk in the door or receive a text message the following day saying how they loved seeing me and how I always lifted their spirits. Or some would try to schedule my time for the next two to three days to experience the high our interaction had provided them. Flattered and appreciative of their compliments, I found pleasure in knowing I had encouraged them. I was aware I never received the equivalent fulfillment in most of my relationships, but the necessity for community and friendship kept me connected.

Too often, we lug around our baggage like a trophy. We tell ourselves we should be angry at the injustice done to us. We walk through life blaming the world for our problems. We can't blame our parents because they aren't responsible for us anymore. We are grown. It's not the fault of the person who cut you off at the drive-thru that your life sucks. We say, "But you don't understand what I've been through. Try to walk a day in my shoes." Thus, we throw down affirmations like "Well, I get to be like this because such and such happened to me." When we arm ourselves with self-harming truths, we do ourselves a disservice and condemn ourselves to a life of adversity and hardship.

The truth is, unhealed people attract unhealed people, and unhealed people behave in unhealed ways. Healed people attract healed people, and healed people spread genuine love and kindness to themselves and others. Love conquers fear, and learning to love oneself is the first part of the puzzle.

Unfortunately, I hadn't yet grasped that at this point in my life. I often told those in my life how life was meant to be enjoyed, and we only have one life to live. I had the whole song and dance on repeat. But I never permitted myself to let down my hair and breathe. Instead, I managed my life and home, running it like a fine-tuned machine while the unhealed trauma and negative emotions turned rancid within me. I endeavored to excel at everything I touched. If I set a goal, I accomplished it. If I didn't understand something, I would spend hours researching or enroll in a class. The thought of being at a disadvantage by not understanding something or not being in control of my life terrified me. But of course this is an illusion, because we can never truly understand every aspect of life, nor can we control it. It's utterly impossible. We encounter avoidable anxiety and stress when we are constantly peering around the corner to see what is ahead, or keeping one foot in the past by using prior struggles and experiences to define our future.

In dissecting ourselves and what makes us tick, we can start our journey toward healing. The choice is ours. Remain stuck in the mud of your past, blaming your failures and who you have or haven't become on your parents and others who you believe have harmed you, and I promise you, it will get you nowhere. To heal, we rise by taking an honest look at ourselves, at our story, the one we have on repeat. We are required to sort through the illusions and the truth to heal. In examining our past and our present with a clear vision, we're required to scrutinize the good and the bad.

In the beginning chapters, I focus on the darkness before revealing the light in future chapters.

In releasing blame, anger, shame, and guilt and downloading new programming with a healthy, positive platform, I've come to appreciate the beauty in the little things.

I cut myself some slack and laugh more. I dance around the house with my dogs and act silly. In good humor, and not at their expense, I tease my husband, children, and friends. My outer appearance doesn't have to be perfect. I don't need to say just the right thing. I don't need to know everything in life. It's okay to be authentically me. The liberation is exhilarating. And there's nothing as liberating as a good old belly laugh. It gets the positive energy moving and is indeed food for the soul.

6–LURKING

"Love is the supreme form of communication. In the hierarchy of needs, love stands as the supreme developing agent of the humanity of the person. As such, the teaching of love should be the central core of all early childhood curriculum with all other subjects growing naturally out of such teaching." ~
Ashley Montagu

In fifth grade, my father moved the family to Tennessee, and I recall my excitement mixed with the uncertainty of what waited outside the small world I'd known. But despondency soon overshadowed the grand adventure as my parents rehomed our family pets.

One of our cats had gone missing days before, and as we drove away, distress overcame me as fear of what would become of him set in.

As we settled in our new home, an old southern mansion, my mother's fears of snakes and poison ivy restricted our ability to play. Our discovery of a hissing snake in the middle of the upstairs floor didn't help the matter. But, as country kids, we were used to coming in and out, and remaining indoors felt restricting.

Our new home was next to the railroad tracks, and on the other side was the state prison. While my parents were away visiting friends, we older girls, aged between eleven and fourteen, were left to mind the younger ones. A convict escaped from the prison, and I recall his orange jumpsuit as he raced from the front door to the windows, trying to get into the house.

Another day, I stood at the living room window and watched, horrified, as a Chow Chow threw a cat in the air, over and over, killing the animal.

The bad doesn't outshine the good in our time spent there. My fondest memory comes with our landlord. He owned several stores, and sometimes our parents would send us older girls to the outbuildings to help unload shipments of shoes and candy. Our reward was a fistful of candy or a new pair of shoes. One pair I chose were snakeskin, each with a shiny buckle on the toe. I'm sure my mother appreciated that. Never having had such luxuries before, we proudly marched home with the bounty of our hard work.

All the changes in our lives—a different church, new people, a new home, and an unfamiliar environment—became a stimulation overload, and any sense of novelty soon wore off.

My father owned a hunting resort in Canada, and as hunting season rolled around, he returned to run his business, leaving us behind in the care of my mother.

Today fear encompasses every aspect of her life, and she struggles to deal with mundane tasks. I can only imagine the crippling anxiety she felt when left to care for seven children in a new place. As a child, I never felt secure in her handling of situations or in her capabilities. She never took on the role of mother and protector, but more of a sibling.

My father's leaving disrupted my world, and for days I felt panicked and physically ill. For years, I never understood why I experienced such agony from his leaving. Later, in my teen years,

I welcomed the times he was away on business. I've come to recognize how deeply his dictatorship had affected me. In his absence, I feared everything would fall apart. I experienced the same panic with his death. I was happily married for fourteen years by then and had created a successful life for myself as a mother, wife, and entrepreneur. I kept my parents and their opinions at bay. However, his death turned my world upside down and sent me reeling, as though I couldn't manage my life without him, despite never allowing him to dictate to me after I left home. Even then, his reach still touched me because childhood conditioning lingered. I had learned that he was a dictator and next to God. His wrath transcended my fear of the external being we were taught about in church. He governed the house and our lives like a drill sergeant. My heart jumped and raced when he entered a room, or when I heard his voice. When he said "Jump," I jumped. If he said "Run," I ran.

I understood, as a child, that he was the one who made things happen at home. He provided shelter and food, and when he returned to Canada I couldn't function. During his absence, I remember climbing into my parents' empty bed, trying to find comfort, but to no avail.

During this time, a girl from church asked if I could come to a sleepover. To my surprise and distress, my mother agreed. You'd think the chance to be a kid and go on a sleepover would've made me happy, but instead, it fueled me with anxiety. In the following days leading up to the sleepover, nausea chased me. I paced the floors and watched the ticking clock. I repeatedly begged my mother to let me stay home, but she made me go. In her neglect to comfort me and quell my distress, I've wondered if my mother's incessant need to keep up appearances made her force me to attend the sleepover.

I eyed the family on the ride to their house warily, feeling small and out of place. Then, as I walked into their house, my barriers rose, and I retreated inward. Like a frightened, cornered animal seeking an escape, I observed my surroundings, scanning for who or what prowled in the shadows.

My friend's family was lovely, and I recollect the kindness in her mother's brown eyes, but I expected her to attack.

I followed after my friend as she showed me around, feeling out of sorts and numb. When it was time for bed, my panic and nausea intensified. I lay alert most of the night, drifting off from time to time before jerking awake to lie vigilant.

The next day couldn't come fast enough. Although the family had welcomed me into their home and showed me nothing but kindness, I felt an urgency to get back to the cocoon and safety of my home. Regardless of what life at home entailed, I associated home with a deluded sense of safety.

When my parents could no longer afford to live in the south, we had to return home. Our toys and belongings were placed in one of the outbuildings. Sadness gripped me as our minivan, loaded to the brim with children and what little would fit inside, drove past the building on our way out. For years, I reminisced about all my things left behind.

In adulthood, taking care of my things and creating a home and a sacred space held great importance. I can see how experiences have impressed these requirements upon me.

When I became pregnant with my son at twenty-one, I promised him and myself that I would make our home a haven, that he'd never fear walking through the door, and he'd know what unconditional love was.

The bond with your firstborn is like no other. A fierce lioness reared within me as he developed in the womb. I vowed to love and protect him, and to provide him with a home life I never had.

Now my son is twenty-two, a university student, and living at home. I say with good humor and the deepest affection that perhaps I made our home too comfortable.

He is a beautiful old soul with wisdom beyond his years. And when I'm in the tenderness of his embrace and see the love radiating in his eyes when he looks at me, I know I created a sacred space for my son to thrive.

However, I mothered two children. A son and a daughter. Children are unique, and although born into the same family, they require individual approaches. A lesson I learned in raising my daughter.

Her struggles in the public school system and the damage created to her psyche presented us with many challenges. And at times, the trauma from my husband and I influenced our parenting of her, which I'll address later.

Stepping-Stone Exercises

In this chapter, I spoke a lot about the sanctuary of your home, the environment, and the importance therein. Our sense of safety and security comes with having our basic physical and emotional needs met. Unfortunately, as children, some of us never had these basic needs satisfied. With our foundation jeopardized, we enter our adult years weighed down with insecurities, anxiety, and fear.

Having a safe environment to retreat to at the end of the day to unwind is vital. Ask yourself, does going home fill me with distress and anxiety? If so, what in your environment is the cause?

Is it your spouse or partner? Your children? Or maybe your home is filled with clutter and chaos.

I, for one, don't thrive in a home filled with uproar and turmoil. An argument between my husband and I, my children, or other family members will send me into a downhill spiral of distress.

I can't stress enough the importance of creating sacred space for you in your life. We are the creators of our lives. We are in control. However, often we give our power away to others in our lives or by remaining stuck in the past.

It is time to get rid of toxic people in your life. Perhaps there's a friend or family member who's become a parasite, mooching off you mentally or financially. Reserve your energy and set healthy boundaries. After all, how can you show up in your life if you have nothing left to give yourself?

It's time to do some housekeeping. Create an environment that betters your everyday life. Take charge of your personal life, starting with the people in it and your home. A sink overloaded with dirty dishes or heaps of dirty or unfolded laundry can make you feel like you're drowning. Fill your home and environment with love, peace, and cleanliness. There's no better time than now to declutter and to create sacred space in your life. Take those old clothes you don't wear and donate them to charity. Have that garage sale you've been saying you're going to have for years. Clean out that junk drawer or room you hurry to hide things in before the guests arrive. (We all have one!) Open the windows and air the house out.

I believe the condition of our home speaks to how we feel inside. If your life is filled with stress and chaos and you're overwhelmed, your home will reflect it. The same goes for a life of happiness and contentment.

If we reprogram our brain to think of tasks we've considered chores as therapeutic, we find pleasure. Small changes, in time, reap massive rewards. If you don't make your bed each morning, start. It's amazing how folding back the covers and climbing into a made bed will make you feel at the end of the day.

A work environment is equally important. If at first you can't change your work environment, start at home. Your home is your castle. We spend a considerable part of our lives there. It's time to gift yourself with establishing a healthy foundation. Set yourself up for success.

7—THE CLEANSING

"Shame loves secrecy. The most dangerous thing to do after a shaming experience is hide or bury our story. When we bury our story, the shame metastasizes." ~ **Brené Brown**

As mentioned in a previous chapter, my father was an avid hunter and had a resort where Americans came to hunt and fish. Hence, climbing off the school bus and seeing animals hanging from posts, gutted and waiting to be skinned, was my norm.

My dad made his own bullets and flies for fly fishing in the attic of our old farmhouse. Mom and Dad constantly warned my little sisters of the danger of playing in there. However, kids being kids, they never heeded the warnings, and one day Dad found them playing with the gunpowder.

My memory of the incident is fragmented; I don't recall the beating taking place, but I remember the shape and color of the curtain rod. One of my duties was to bathe the four little girls, and later that day or maybe the next, I remember standing over the tub looking down at their naked bodies. My throat tightened, and I stood numb; a sense of powerlessness enveloped me as I observed the bruises marring their bodies. *Why?* Tortured my mind. I couldn't understand the rationale. He hadn't wanted them hurt by playing in the gunpower, but hadn't the thrashing caused more harm?

Merriam-Webster dictionary defines beating as "an act of striking with repeated blows to injure or damage." Regarding my upbringing, I define a spanking and a beating as two very different acts. A spanking smarted, but it never broke you the way the beatings did. I know much of the world supports spankings, but I don't. How can you possibly teach a child a helpful and productive lesson with aggression? How do you teach a dog not to pee on the floor by driving the animal's nose into it? You can't! It's ludicrous to think you can. These acts instill fear of the perpetrator and the pain that comes with it. It may teach a child not to step out of line, and both child and animal will learn to cower, but for the perpetrator, it's to demonstrate who's more powerful.

My fear of inappropriate discipline, along with the concern my husband would use the wrong word choice, causing damage to my children's psyches, caused me to restrain him when it came to raising our children. Over the years, I protested at how he never helped raise them. In addition, my husband struggled with lack from his childhood. He feared not having enough money to support his family and was determined his family would never go without; work became his first marriage, leaving me to feel like a single parent, alone and unsupported. When I remember our parenting years, I have to be honest and admit I stole his power to be wholly involved when he was around. I didn't trust him to parent—not because of him, but because I never trusted myself. What if I damaged my kids? What if I said the wrong thing? What if I hurt them like my parents had me? The agony of such thoughts tormented me.

The responsibility of being someone's parent scared the life out of me. How could I captain a ship of passengers when I didn't possess the confidence or have the guidance to make it to shore? As a result, I second-guessed every step of my parenting. In my determination to do better than my parents, I aimed to be anything but them. With this vow, I could never be free of my parents and their mistakes in raising us girls. If I'd trusted myself more and the parent I had proven to be, I would've gained confidence in my love and my sensitivity to my children's well-being and not battled the anxiety of becoming my parents.

My dad's way of showing us love came with physical aggression and, at times, cruelty. My mother also behaved with hostility at times, but her attempts to manage us by applying pain didn't happen often. Besides the odd times when she punched me in the side of the head out of frustration, or took my head and repeatedly banged it against the wall, hers never hurt physically because she didn't have the physical power to put behind it. It was my mother's neglect and responses that broke my heart.

As a child, I believed that my sisters and I were the problem because, if there weren't so many of us, my parents wouldn't feel overwhelmed and stressed. It cost a lot to raise a family of our size, and I was aware of the financial struggle. I recall scouring the house and looking between couch cushions for change to buy butter. Times were hard in the early days. I know my dad worked hard to provide for his family. He found any job necessary until he started his own business in my preteen years.

My parents were unhealed and not prepared to take on seven children. As a result, our household was lacking in guidance, nurturing, and protection. The overflow of responsibilities landed on the older children's shoulders; mostly my oldest sister's and mine, as my second-oldest sister spent her time studying.

When my oldest sister turned thirteen, it was like my parents stepped back and left the four younger girls' rearing to us. My oldest sister, however, had the burden of being in charge. My heart breaks for the weight she must have felt. A thirteen-year-old is hardly capable of managing a household and six children. When we cut up, she tried to discipline us the way my parents did, with the belt or whatever object she could find. Often frustrated and overwhelmed, she resorted to my mother's threat of reporting us to Dad when he got home. Implanting the fear of Dad was all she needed to put us in order.

As mentioned, one of my duties was bathing my younger sisters. I never had a lot of patience for the task because my sisters' hair had never been cut and extended to their waists or longer. It was a chore and a half to bathe them. I'd leave them in the shower while I went to fetch towels, instructing them to get their hair wet so I could apply the shampoo when I returned. I'd come back, and they'd be huddled in the farthest corner of the shower with not a lick of water on them. I'd haul them under the water, and they'd kick up a fuss while I reprimanded them for being a pain. I earned the nickname "Bull Moose" because I often chased them to round them up for bath time, dressing, or combing their hair. Anger at my mother for not taking care of her responsibilities fueled me, and I know my younger sisters suffered from my frustration.

We older girls were but children ourselves. We didn't possess the affection and wisdom healthy parents would have offered under stress. Shame and guilt over how I lashed out at my younger sisters plagued me for years.

Stepping-Stone Exercises

What secret or shame rests at your core? So often, we're haunted and weighed down with guilt over things we can't go back and change. It is time to forgive yourself.

Punishing yourself for something you did will keep you from living a quality life, rich in love and happiness. You must acknowledge your shortcomings and release them. You're not meant to carry that cross for the rest of your life. That is Old School mentality. So many times we've heard people say, "You should be ashamed of yourself." It's been schooled into us. And it's time we school it out.

Shaming is not the way. We are a more evolved society, with proper tools to self-heal. Don't remain under the thumb of guilt and shame. Don't waste another day punishing yourself. You deserve to be free. You deserve to love, be loved, and give love. And, most importantly, this love needs to extend to you.

Write down what you have held over your own head, and how it has held you back in your life and relationships. Through your words, tell the inner child within you that you forgive them. Don't edit! Let the words and the emotions flow. Being vulnerable is beautiful, and in this exercise, the only one that sees your vulnerability is you. It is safe. Find your release. You deserve it.

When you've finished, tear the page out and roll it up. I had a firepit outside when I made my forgiveness note to myself, but you can also use your sink. Burn the letter, and as you watch the flame ignite, taking with it the shame and guilt, place a hand to your heart and look to the heavens and say, aloud or mentally," I forgive myself."

Well done, beautiful soul! You have rewarded yourself with a beautiful gift that no one else could ever give you. Your future just got a little brighter.

8–IMAGINATION

"I did spend a lot of time as a child very confused about whether I had a devil in me, or whether I was in a state of grace. I mean, these ideas are so potent to anybody with half an imagination." ~ **Antony Gormley**

One day my sisters and I spent hours digging, trying to find the devil. I wanted to see this demon that tormented my life and caused me so much anguish. My imagination ran wild at what would happen when he reached from the earth and grabbed me, but I didn't care; I needed to see him for myself. As we dug, we chatted about how we'd have to dig to China first because, in our young minds, China was far away. At this time, we hadn't been far from the property we were raised on, so once we reached China, hell would surely be nearby. Eventually, we abandoned the mission.

As children, we didn't have a lot of free time to play and be kids. We worked hard, often from dusk to dark. Our farmhouse had a wood-burning furnace. After we got home from school in the colder months, we'd have to chip away the ice to get the outer wood door open to carry wood into the cellar for the furnace. I pledged to never own a wood-burning fireplace when I got older because of the amount of wood we hauled and piled. My dad would order us to stack the wood on one side of the house, and when the task was done he would tell us to start over and move it to another side of the house. We would grumble but do as he requested. I believe it was his way of keeping us out of their hair. I used to get excited when it would start to get dark because I wanted to be done working, but then he had a streetlight installed, so darkness falling held no hope of a break.

I learned to live inside my head. It was there where I created an imaginary world and withdrew from my reality. Movies or TV shows became an outlet for me. I imagined myself as the characters and living a life outside my small world. Depending on my parents' convictions at the time, we watched monitored TV programs with them. I remember the cable cord being woven through the open register, from the attic to the main floor. Disney used to have a program that played on Sundays, and my parents let us watch it. I looked forward to it all week. Then, sometime later, which could be weeks, the cord and TV disappeared, and I knew it had been taken away because it was evil. It would reappear, and then disappear, until the day Dad took the TV outside and shot it with a shotgun, claiming it was of the devil. I looked on with a broken heart.

Dad loved the Old West. He had boxes of Louis L'Amour and Zane Grey books, but reading wasn't my thing back then, so when movies were permitted I found the same escape others found in books. When a new screen arrived in the house, my dad rented old westerns often featuring Clint Eastwood, or watched the TV series *Five Mile Creek*, set in the 1800s in the Outback. Two of the main characters were best friends, named Maggie and Kate. Kate was feisty and could hold her own in a time when women had little say. I admired her and longed to be just like her. I dreamed of having a voice in the world. On the other hand,

Maggie was prim and proper, and I had had my fill of that. But she had spunk. She forwent women's apparel in one show and marched through town in pants with her chin held high.

Dad also loved the Deep South, so often, we watched those types of movies. I felt connected to those in bondage on the plantations. Although my life could never compare to their anguish, I related to the abuse, powerlessness, and lack of freedom they endured. Rage simmered in my chest at the injustice I saw placed on humanity. My heart soared when they took their chance and raced toward the promise of freedom, and in my mind, I raced right along with them. *One day I will find my freedom*, I promised myself. *I won't live in fear. My voice will matter. I will have the privilege of speech and think for myself. If they can break free, so can I.* Their plight and courage gave me hope. They become my heroes, and at night I lay awake thinking of them, and throughout the day, I lived in a world with these characters inside my head.

Throughout my adolescence, my parents' convictions were all over the place. Selected video games were allowed, and then not. Christmas was okay one year, and the next it was a pagan holiday. My parents' paradox added heaps of confusion and left me spinning on unsteady ground. What was right, and what was wrong?

As an adult, I took a broader view and put into perspective that my parents were human too. They didn't have life all figured out either. They were conflicted in their faith and in themselves as people. With this reflection, I released the hurt and frustration at the dysfunction. I can look back and see my parents were doing the best they knew how. The mere fact that sometimes they used the little money they had to purchase video games or rent movies for us was their way of bringing joy to our lives.

9–NURTURANCE

"When infants aren't held, they can become sick, even die. It's universally accepted that children need love, but at what age are people supposed to stop needing it? We never do. We need love in order to live happily, as much as we need oxygen in order to live at all." ~ **Marianne Williamson**

From the time I had my first menstrual cycle, I've suffered from painful periods. I would take showers in the middle of the night, trying to ease the pain and other symptoms that came with it. My periods were so bad my mother took me to the doctor to see what could be done. He suggested birth control pills, but my mother refused. Next, Advil was suggested, but my mother also rebuffed that advice, informing me she had read somewhere that Advil could cause flesh-eating disease. I would experience the extent of her fears throughout my childhood and adult years. She often recited from the Bible in her children's times of worry: "Well, what Job feared came upon him." Then she would go on to tell you of the afflictions he suffered, starting with the open sores, then losing three daughters and seven sons, his wealth, or however the story goes. It became her way of silencing us. Yet she never seemed to personally apply the quote because she lived in a constant state of anxiety, worry, and fear.

When we were growing up, she was notorious for absorbing all the horrors in the media and relating them to us children. She would tell us of the rapists, pedophiles, or murderers at large throughout our childhood—I recall her telling me a horrendous story about someone chopping up their baby and putting it in the microwave. These stories disturbed me and made me more afraid of the outside world.

In tenth grade, the pain from my monthly cycle had become so bad that I called home, hoping my mother would come to get me. I didn't like school any more than I liked going home. I often recall riding the bus home and praying that my dad wouldn't be there when I arrived home. Once in my teen years, I remember daydreaming of his plane crashing when he was away on business and him not returning. I shook my head to dislodge the thought while experiencing heaps of guilt and shame. I felt like a terrible person for wishing my father's death, though it wasn't his death I wanted but the anxiety, fear, and abuse to end.

When I called home that day, the worst possible person answered. As I heard Dad's "hello" on the other end of the phone, my gut sank. I quickly asked for my mother because she was the lesser of the two evils, in my mind. I didn't fear her. But she was away somewhere, and because of the amount of discomfort I was in, I decided I'd take the risk of going home. I longed to climb into bed with a hot water bottle or take a shower to ease the pain. I informed him I was sick and needed to come home. To my dismay, he told me I could come home, but when I did, I had to work.

At home, our guests had finished lunch and retired to their lodgings. I cleared the table and stood at the sink, washing the pile of dishes while feeling miserable and ready to collapse at any moment.

Nurturance was a rarity. Physical touch in any positive light was something I don't remember. The same goes for my parents offering words of comfort, and the guidance they attempted to offer came with rebuke and the need to instill fear. Likewise, hugs and kisses and expressions of love are simply something I don't remember. I was married with two kids the first time I recall my parents saying, "I love you." It felt awkward but good at the same time.

Today my mother will say she loves you, but it is rare and doesn't flow naturally from her. My conversations with her are over the phone and are very superficial. I've always been one who prefers deeper and more meaningful discussions; I have little time for idle chitchat. I rarely touch on profound subjects with her, not because she isn't intelligent, but because she likes to keep conversations shallow. She is notorious for being defensive, blaming and shaming you, shutting down, and dismissing your emotions. As a result, we are two very different people, and I have difficulty relating to her.

Pleasant conversations that leave you uplifted seldom happen with her. Therefore, I limit our interactions. I've discovered that expressing how you feel isn't safe with her. While writing this book, I called her. As usual, I half listened during the call while she talked about all the news and her fears of every possible illness and horrible outcome. She proceeded to inquire about an acquaintance, and not wanting to discuss others, I quickly said the person was evolving and went on to say how inspired I was by them. Then I shifted the conversation to relate how we're all capable of transformation, how I'd changed so much in the last decade, and how free I felt. I noted the change in her breathing; I'd surpassed her comfort zone. However, I disregarded the red flags and went on to say that I used to cringe when friends embraced me because it wasn't something I was accustomed to. The conversation, which had been tolerable, took a drastic turn.

She shouted into the other end of the phone, "I hugged you, Naomi. When you were little."

The insult and anger were evident in her tone. I had struck a nerve. Years ago, the unhealed me would've absorbed her reaction. I would've shouldered the blame for the negative shift in the conversation, believing I had upset her; therefore, it was my fault. I would have shut down and retreated or spent the next several minutes recanting my words. But instead, as she went off on a tangent, I held the phone away from my ear. This has become habitual in my communications with her. Especially when she reverts to bouts of victim mentality and venting the unhealed places inside her on me.

My mother's defensiveness severed the flow of the conversation. I disengaged. After she'd finished her rant, I told her it wasn't about her, that it was merely a statement, nothing more. Then, after her voice returned to an even level, I spoke for a minute or so more, and I wished her a good day and excused myself from the conversation.

As she asserted, she may have shown affection in the early years, but I remember not liking the feel of her skin or her touch in my preteen and teenage years. As an adult, I know it had nothing to do with the feeling of her skin because her skin is soft. But as a child, I understood she did not see or hear me. My needs didn't register with her. Therefore, I didn't find any solace or refuge in her. The knowledge that I found her touch repulsive filled me with shame and disgust at myself. How could I feel that way about my own mother? What was wrong with me?

∽

One winter, when my father was away on business, my mother, siblings, and I came down with the flu. I remember huddling around the wood stove, our only source of heat, trying to stay warm. I recall the sense of bonding that came from all of us having the flu—we were all in it together. And with Dad gone, the cloak of fear had lifted. I felt permission to be sick without worrying about being judged lazy, or the need to scramble around to please or avoid him.

Uprooting the idea that downtime or recovery is lazy has been a massive struggle for me. However, removing the belief that life is intended to be hard and that achieving success required me to constantly jump through hoops gave me the freedom to breathe and live a more quality existence.

Throughout the years, my sisters and I have had in-depth conversations about our upbringing. Some remember wanting to be sick so that they could get attention. I can't relate to these childhood feelings because I've always dreaded being sick. However, once or twice in adulthood, I recall a similar thought coming to mind before I quickly brushed it away, disturbed that I could be so needy that I'd contemplate being sick for love and attention.

An old acquaintance I had once faked throat cancer for attention, and I remember being disgusted and astonished that she would do such a thing. I believed she was playing with fire.

Concerned over why I had considered sickness in order to be seen and heard, albeit briefly, I had to question why it'd come up in the first place. I wanted to get to the root. My rational brain grasped that I didn't want to get sick, and I certainly didn't want to die. The fear of death followed me most of my life. No one wants to suffer or be sick, but it went deeper than that for me. I feared what came after death, and if my parents' and the church's teachings of hell were warranted. I avoided discussing death and illnesses, or dwelling on topics of that sort. I evade people when they come down with the flu. My friends have laughed at me because, when they've been ill, I've been known to deliver soup, ginger ale, and Gravol to their doorstep before ringing the bell and quickly stepping a safe distance back to avoid germs.

My craving for a gentle physical touch was apparent throughout my life. At one point in my childhood, I came up with the idea that my little sisters could pamper me, and I'd pay them. I rarely had access to money, but I hunted all over the house for a quarter. Once a deal was struck for their services, they pretended they were my nurses. They brought me water in a cup, representing medicine, and checked my temperature before running away to retrieve a cool cloth for my forehead. The gentleness of their hands helped me to relax, and in these moments, I felt loved and cared for. Yet the memory of me paying them to comfort me felt wrong and shameful. The depths of the shame and my uneasiness with the memory would take years to discover.

When my kids were toddlers, I would take them for a nap in my bed and soothe them by gently stroking their back, ears, and hair. Eventually they started saying, "Mommy, play with my ears and hair" at nap time. When my daughter had a rough day as a teenager, she'd climb into my bed and ask me to soothe her as I'd done when she was a child. In later years, she'd smile and say, in a nostalgic tone, "Remember when you used to take us for naps in your bed? You would rub our backs or play with our ears and hair until we fell asleep."

I extended the same soothing technique to my husband in bed at night, until we both fell asleep. The calming motions soothed me as much as they did him.

Physical touch and allowing others to be in my personal

space was limited to my children and husband. It all came down to trust. I knew they loved me, and my husband had earned my trust, which allowed me to let down my guard to let them close enough.

When my daughter was little, she'd watch me with interest as I applied my makeup. Her bright blue eyes widened and narrowed with each stroke of the brush, and she asked endless questions about the application. As her interest grew, she began to ask if she could try putting makeup on me. Finally, one day I gave in and sat down to let her work her magic. Her being small and not knowing how to apply it, I usually looked like a clown when she was done. I smile when I recall how she would stand back and admire her work before handing me the mirror to look for myself. I would laugh and tell her what a good job she'd done.

Sometimes my son, who's two years older, thought it'd be fun and joined in. With their combined creativity, they transformed me into a tiger, bunny, or whatever appealed to them that day. Concern over them wasting my expensive cosmetics faded as I listened to their happy chatter, and as I had with my sisters, I relaxed into the care of their trusted hands. I soaked up their attention and love.

One day, my son took it a step further and wanted to add his own creative flair. He decided he wanted to paint tattoos on me and showed up with his pencil case full of markers. At first I objected because I worried about the harm of absorbing chemicals, but I gave in and allowed him to make sleeve tattoos. Often, I'd doze off under the gentleness of their touch.

It wasn't long before my son tired of being an amateur tattoo artist and went back to his video games. However, my daughter was accustomed to going on mother-and-daughter dates with me to the spa for pedicures, facials, and manicures. She loved to paint my nails and style my hair. I have a bald spot over my left eyebrow where she burned me with the flat iron. I was a sucker for punishment, but quickly decided I didn't want to be anywhere near my eleven-year-old with a straightener in her hand. Eventually, she created at-home spa days for me and made coupons for the treatments she provided at her spa. I flipped through the coupons looking for one I had the patience for that wouldn't result in a big mess for me to clean up after. I smiled with endearment at the misspelled words and loads of hearts. Her love and desire to do something nice for me are revealed in her effort.

I still have some of those coupons and the little bag of cinnamon heart candies she gave me at one treatment. Last year, I texted her a picture of the coupons and the bag of candy, telling her I may still cash in.

For a time, she wanted to pamper me every other week or month. Although I enjoyed the spoiling, guilt soon set in because I felt I was using her. So I suggested paying her for her services, as one would at an actual spa. She eagerly agreed and went so far as to give her one-client business a name. But unfortunately her prices rose, as they often do in business. At the hefty price of $50, I decided to stick to the professionals. I've often wondered why I felt ashamed and bothered paying my little sisters and my child for these pampering sessions. Had I done something morally wrong? Was it because I was an adult and felt like I had taken advantage of them? Was I enforcing child labor? At a quarter, my little sisters may have considered it so.

All silliness aside, I dove deeper into the emotions. I considered why, when I asked my husband to let me lie on his lap and for him to play with my hair to help me relax before sleep, I didn't get that nagging in my gut. In the early years of our marriage, when I couldn't afford to get a pedicure or manicure, I got my husband to paint my nails. He didn't like it any, but he'd do it for me. As soon as we could afford for me to go to the spa, though, he retired. During this exchange of energy, he showed me kindness, love, and affection, and I surrendered myself into his considerate hands, and my body and mind calmed. I never paid him for his devotion and love, but I felt bad that I had made him do something he didn't enjoy that used his free time.

I craved the magic in my loved one's hands: the love, affection, calmness, and safety I acquired.

Letting people within my personal space had become an obstacle. I never found getting my hair done or getting pedicures and manicures by professionals enjoyable or relaxing. It was something I endured because I wanted to look nice. Estheticians would constantly tell me to relax because I made their job laborious. I attempted to limit how much control they had over my physical body. When I started suffering from chronic neck and hip pain in my thirties, I sought a chiropractor. To my dismay, I was assigned a male chiropractor, and because of my experience with a male general practitioner at nineteen, which I will touch on later, I felt nervous. So, before going, I googled videos of what takes place during treatment to gain control and knowledge of what to expect. I felt stressed waiting in the room for him to come in because I knew he'd be in my personal space while maneuvering my body for treatment. Although, at this point in my life, I had no issues with getting up and walking out if I thought something was off, I recall sitting in the room telling myself I should've refused the appointment and asked for a female. Then he waltzed into the room with his charismatic personality and easy way, and I relaxed a tad. But still, during the adjustment,

I ended up giggling throughout the whole treatment because it felt incredibly awkward to have him in my personal space. For those of you who have been to a chiropractor, you know how much trust it requires to allow them to adjust you. You are vulnerable to their experience and ability.

Despite the awkwardness of that first appointment, he was my chiropractor for years because I learned to trust him. When we moved to a new province, I had to find another chiropractor, and he, too, is male. Because I've been known to try to control the adjustments, I've learned that by closing my eyes and reminding myself that I am safe, I can relax into the care of the professional.

Until my midthirties, I would never go for massages. First off, lying naked on a table was one impediment, and second, allowing someone to put their hands on me was another. A massage felt too vulnerable.

My trainers at the gym would get agitated at me because I held my breath when performing the circuits and cardio. I love yoga because it helps me relax, and yoga lovers know the practice is all about strength, flexibility, and mind-body awareness. However, for years, I'd get light-headed. Then I realized I was holding my breath during the poses, and only when we switched positions would I release my breath. I also enjoy hiking and being in nature, and my lungs would feel like they were going to burst within minutes of climbing a mountain or a hill—again I realized I was holding my breath to power through.

I had learned to hold my breath. Especially when it came to beatings and receiving physical punishment, which required the punisher to be within my personal space. So, as I had learned to do during the belt games, I'd brace and hold my breath in hopes of easing the pain and difficulty.

As a child and well into my adult years, I released deep sighs to ease stress and anxiety. I observed the exact coping mechanism in my daughter and understood why. However, my parents thought I was rebellious and scolded me for it.

When I was a teenager, I recall standing at the cupboard, and my dad walking up and reaching for something in an upper cabinet near me, and instinctively, I cowered, put my hands up to protect myself, and held my breath. Outraged, he rebuked me for my behavior. And, as usual, I grasped I had done something wrong and bore the blame.

One of the last beatings I received was when I was around eighteen years of age. I don't remember what my crime was, but my father told me to lean over the bed with my hands out in front. Everything in me wanted to rebel, but fear bent my body into submission. But my mind never gave in. I was determined I would not show weakness. I would not give him the satisfaction of seeing me cry because I knew that was his goal. As the first lash came, I swallowed my cry while reciting in my head, *Don't cry. Stay strong.* The lashes kept coming, and as I felt my spirit breaking, I distracted myself by thinking of the ankle-length rust skirt with teal and orange flowers and the light-colored top I wore. I held out for a while longer, but the power behind his blows soon buckled my knees, and I fell face-first into the bed, weeping and broken and hoping it was over. But then he told me it would continue until I gained control of myself.

Sometime around this time, I came home from school and found flowers on my bed. My heart leaped at the surprise, and for a moment, I felt delighted because gifts didn't come often, and I'd never received flowers before. Flowers felt so grown-up. Then I asked my mother who they were from, and she informed me my dad had purchased them for me. I went cold inside and considered his motive and what price I would pay to earn the flowers.

In reflection, I realized how I had been conditioned to believe that obtaining love and attention came at a cost. A pattern that would play out in the endless amounts of money I gave to family and friends. To earn love and friendship, there was a price.

∽

Learning to self-soothe has been a process but it has been instrumental in my healing. Your power lies in calming the mind. Therapy scratches at the surface of the emotions and trauma, but in my experience, it never provided the tools to manage the mind. In calming my mind and practicing self-soothing techniques, I gained freedom from anxiety.

There was an incident some time into the process of me learning to calm my mind, where my husband and I had errands to run, but I had an appointment first, and he missed the turnoff. I started to panic inside because I dreaded being late. I never wanted to upset the other person, and believed it was disrespectful. Respect for others and their time is important to me. After all, what you give out, you receive in return.

However, I quickly noticed the panic start to build this day and knew I could ease it. I closed my eyes, and took some depth breaths, and told myself, "I will get there when I do. There is nothing I can do to control my arrival time, and that is perfectly okay. Everything will be okay."

I opened my eyes and realized the anxiety had floated away, as though I had simply snapped my fingers. Yes, it is that easy. I applied the self-soothing and breathing techniques I had learned and calmed my mind.

The mind is powerful. And I've witnessed its power on several occasions, which I will share with you later.

Morning Practice to Aid in Your Journey

Peeling back the layer of trauma is an essential step in healing. It's equally important to free yourself from various trauma symptoms such as anxiety, depression, chronic neck and back pain, migraines, inflammation, etc. Dr. Bessel van der Kolk speaks about the effects of trauma in his book, *The Body Keeps the Score*. His book is brilliant, and I highly recommend it.

I have a self-love morning practice that sets my day up for success. I can't imagine my life without it, and I strongly suggest you create one that works for you. Mine takes about thirty minutes, but you can make yours shorter. Start with five minutes and adapt to fit your schedule. Everyone has five to ten minutes in the course of the day, and time spent on yourself is invaluable.

I start my day with a glass of water and add 1/8 teaspoon of Celtic salt to rehydrate. Then, I go to an area in my home that is just for me. I have my yoga mat rolled out in front of a full-length mirror. I light a candle or incense or both before sitting in front of the mirror. Then, I take a moment to admire and appreciate the reflection looking back at me. At first it was difficult to look at myself without judging, but in time, it became easier. Now I smile and tell myself, "I love you. You are amazing. You've got this"—whatever comes to mind at the moment. Then I scan my whole body with appreciation and wonder before thanking it for all it does for me.

After, I do stretches to ease the morning aches and pains. Followed by at least ten minutes of meditation. YouTube has some great meditations. My favorites are by Lavendaire or The Daily Calm. Lavendaire's guided meditation for anxiety and stress has different neck stretches, which helps with shoulder and neck tightness, often caused by stress. It, along with her self-love video, are the ones I do weekly. In time, you will find whose voice and method you prefer. Sometimes I forgo guided meditations and sit with my eyes closed and focus on my breathing. Meditation is excellent for the overactive mind. Let your thoughts come and go. Become aware of the overall tone of your thoughts. Are they negative or positive? Don't judge yourself, but simply let them float away. Your thoughts will give you valuable insight into the condition of your mind.

After I finish, I take out my gratitude journal and write down three to five things I'm grateful for. This proved to be a critical step for me. Practicing gratitude is life-changing. Too often, we focus on all that's going wrong in our lives and forget about all the good. When we change our mindset, we change our world. If at first you can't find something to be grateful for, look down at your hand holding the pen, and give thanks that you can move your fingers. Better yet, that you have sight to see. There is so much we have in life to be grateful for, but we get caught up in a negative frame of mind.

When I take my morning shower, I give thanks for having running water, electricity, and the abundance to afford a roof over my head. When you start seeing life from a place of plenty and not lack, you will find more to be grateful for.

And when you start to appreciate the wonder that looks back at you in the mirror and uproot criticism of yourself and others, joy and happiness will naturally come to you.

You can self-heal. The magic lies within you, and it's been there all along.

10—THE SCAN

"Children believe and internalize what their parents say about them. It is sadistic and destructive for a parent to make repetitive jokes at the expense of a vulnerable child."
~ **Dr. Susan Forward,** *Toxic Parents: Overcoming Their Hurtful Legacy and Reclaiming Your Life*

Aunt Glenda was my maternal grandfather's adoptive mother, and someone whom I regard with fondness. Doctors thought she wouldn't make it until I was born, but she fought for another sixteen years before losing her battle with cancer. She lived thirty minutes away from us, in the town where my parents did their grocery shopping and other business. Everyone loved Aunt Glenda. Like my grandfather, she was a gentle soul. When my mom took us to town, we wouldn't let her pass by her road without putting up a fuss to stop at her house. When we visited her, she would bring out a box of thin ginger-snap cookies. On these visits, she and my mother would chat in the kitchen, and we girls would sit in the living room where she had lots of interesting trinkets, and on occasion, she would put on the TV, and we enjoyed the rare luxury of cartoons.

My father rarely went with us to visit her, but I recall one time after my sisters and I had come down with chicken pox, and I was on the mend, my parents went to town and stopped by her house. I must have been around ten or eleven, and as we walked up to the house, my parents informed me I couldn't go in because I could make her sick. Brokenhearted, I sat on the steps. This is my first recollection of the scan. That day, I wore my favorite faded red polka dot dress.

A pattern unfolded: in my memories, I often remembered what I wore. I never understood why these parts of my memory were so vivid until I connected the dots.

I recall my older sister holding me down, an act that filled me with panic, as punishments often came with being pinned down, and I kicked at her to get her off me. My tennis shoe connected with her face. She released me and fell back, crying. I wore white sneakers with teal polka dots. Another time as I sat in church with a man seated to my left, I felt his eyes on me. I glanced at him to find him studying my private area, and I recall my scan of the outline of my thighs in the emerald-green velvet skirt, and squirming inside, thinking maybe the material of my skirt was too revealing. I thought I'd incited him to look at me improperly.

A common practice in our household, especially for me between the ages of thirteen and eighteen, was my dad instructing me to turn in slow, painstaking circles so he could examine the fit of my clothes. He inspected my body to ensure none of my womanly parts would tempt a man. It felt degrading and as though something about me would cause a man "to fall." Again, experiences like the ones described filled me with toxic shame, feelings of defectiveness, and thoughts that I was dirty. The dresses my mother made for me were sack-like, with no shape or form, to hide my curves.

Occasionally we got new clothes, and I recall when my

mother purchased me a brand-new dress from an actual store. I had admired myself in the mirror and felt more beautiful than I ever had. By my dad's standards, the navy dress with small white flowers was too form-fitting. Part of me knew that, but I'd hoped, for once, I could avoid the inspection or—wishful thinking—I'd gain my father's approval. After all, Mom had deemed it okay.

I proceeded downstairs to endure the examination. My father asked me where I had gotten the dress. I informed him that Mom had bought it. He reprimanded her and told me I could never wear it again.

Another time, when I'd come downstairs wearing a baggy hunter-green T-shirt and an ankle-length emerald-green skirt with white flowers, my dad said, "You look like a slut. Get upstairs and get that changed." I recall looking at the extra material and feeling confused. That statement stung the most.

Finally, I'll share another scan. It came during an examination by a male general practitioner at a walk-in clinic when I was nineteen. The memory of that day in the examination room remains with me. I've never spoken to a physician and asked if his examination was acceptable for a bladder infection. However, I recall the uncanny way the doctor looked at me and my uneasiness in his company. I stated that I had a bladder infection, and it wasn't my first. I informed him I'd had one before, and the medicine the doctor had given me took it away.

He laughed and said, "You aren't going to get away that easy, young lady."

He never brought a female assistant into the room (which may not have been standard practice in the late 90s) before asking me to remove my top to take my blood pressure, then insisted on doing an internal and anal exam. Afterward he asked me to follow him to his office, which took us down a narrow hallway to the back of the clinic. My gut told me it wasn't normal, but I followed him nevertheless. I recall how he sat across from me, looking at me with the same creepy smile he'd worn in the examination room. I don't remember anything after that, or leaving his office. However, I'd worn a button-up denim top and a butter-yellow skirt that day.

After that experience, I did my best to avoid male doctors. Some years later, in my early twenties, I met another young mom, and we became friends. During one conversation, I mentioned my experience with this doctor, and her expression grew knowing. She asked for his name, and I told her the location he worked out of and that I could only recall his last name.

"Oh my god!" She took a step back. "He used to be my family doctor, and he did the same uncomfortable things to me."

I'd pushed away what had happened in his office because I believed it was me overreacting. However, in my experience throughout the years, visits to the doctor for a bladder infection required a urine test, never an examination. Also, they've never taken me into their office afterward.

In discovering myself and peeling back the layers of trauma, I realized how I'd conditioned myself to scan my body when I felt dirty, humiliated, and inadequate.

11–PROTECTION

"Our children are our greatest treasure. They are our future. Those who abuse them tear at the fabric of our society and weaken our nation." ~ **Nelson Mandela**

Fragmented memories came and went, but a night I could never forget, no matter how many times my mother said it never happened, always surfaced. Mom was away for the evening at a women's weight loss meeting. Dad stood at the counter, slicing a loaf of bread. One of my older sisters and I stood beside him, awaiting punishment for something I can't remember. The look on my dad's face was different that time. His eyes were hooded, and weariness pulled at him. He turned, with the knife in hand, and told us to hold out our hands. Too frightened to protest, we did as we were told, and he hit our open hands with the knife. A burning sensation ensued before the blood came. I shrieked and squeezed my hands between my legs to stop the pain. Before I knew what was happening, he grabbed me and rushed me to the bathroom. In his hurry, he didn't turn on the light. I recall the cold water on my hands as he placed them under the tap.

In my distress and terror, I continued to scream, and he shouted at me, "Shut up. Shut up, right now!"

Was it the pain or the sight of blood that terrorized me the most? I don't know. Aside from the daunting memory, I retrieve the image of his face and the expression of pure panic. For years I dismissed the look, marring it with my feelings of anger and bewilderment over how he could've lost control like that. Like, who does that? Only a monster, I told myself. He didn't love me. He couldn't have. I carried the belief that I was unlovable, and there was something about me that my father hated. Something about me he wanted to break.

With reflection and healing, I've accepted he exercised poor judgment, which isn't to be dismissed or downplayed, but if I am to look at the overall picture, I am forced to remember the expression on his face. A sinister person doesn't show empathy and regret. On the contrary, my father was scared and appalled at what he'd done. This, again, doesn't excuse the behavior, but it reveals his realization that he made a ghastly mistake.

My father missed a critical moment to try and rectify that incident, if that is even possible. In the healing process, I've revisited that evening several times and envisioned myself in his shoes. If I put myself in his shoes, and had made a dreadful mistake like that, what would I have done? Each time I would come up with unreasonable solutions. I told myself I would've dropped to my knees, gathered my child in my arms, and told them I was sorry. Then I would beg them to forgive me. As a rational person, I can see that an approach like this would, first off, be self-serving, a way to make myself feel better for what I had done. Second, a child previously groomed to fear a parent would brace or retreat as the parent stepped forward. Perhaps he was aware of that.

But the fantasy of myself/him begging for forgiveness enlightened me to the blame I still bore from that night. I wanted my dad to forgive me because I held the belief he was stressed and worried about life and money, and it was my sister's and my fault; we'd done something to stress him out. So, therefore, we deserved it.

I often considered how an explanation of some sort could've shifted the responsibility I felt to the correct person. But he never mentioned the incident, and my mother denies it. However, my sister and I hold to our truth about what happened that night.

The constant dismissal of the truth about my childhood and the lack of protection made me hypervigilant when it came to my own family. As a result, I adopted a warrior mentality. No one would mess with my family. Although I wasn't a confrontational person by nature, but more of a peacemaker, I prepared for battle when situations I deemed unjust happened to my children or husband. I never used physical violence but used my words. Life had taught me the power of words and to be careful with what I said because words spoken can't be taken back. I wasn't quick to act and often gave myself a night's rest to process the situation in its entirety before acting.

The incessant bullying my youngest child faced in the public school system heightened my hypervigilance. As a parent, it kills you each time you see your child suffer. The neglect of the adults in my childhood charged me with a determination that my children would never feel neglected, alone, or unprotected. If anyone mistreated my children, I stepped up to the plate, ready to take them on while trembling inside and wanting to puke, but I would not see my children harmed. Throughout my daughter's school years I visited the school often, dealing with teachers, principals, and parents so much that I came to dread the start of the school year and relished its end.

The heartache and struggles she went through broke my

heart. I sent her to kindergarten with a skip in her step and eagerness to make friends and learn. However, by grade one, I showed up to pick her up with plastic bags on hand because, at this tender age, she suffered stress migraines that caused her to vomit. As she went from elementary to junior high, I watched her change from the sweet, innocent child I had sent out that first day to one whose eyes were haunted with pain. She became depressed and anxiety-ridden. A heaviness followed her; I could see it resting on her young shoulders. She never slept, dreading the night and the morning that followed. She became hyper-aware of her environment, and on edge. I didn't realize it then, but she had become a vision of me in my childhood. My inner child cried for me to save her.

I did my best to comfort her. I held her and told her all the fantastic and beautiful things about her, attempting to help her self-worth. Her defense was "But you have to say that because you're my mom."

She didn't know the error in her belief because she had two parents who devoted their time and energy to giving her a life filled with love, safety, and guidance. But, nevertheless, her home experience had been very different than her peers'. And, later in her teen years, she'd come to hate the rules we set out for her and long for anything but the home we had created.

The fact is, not all parents are capable of love. Although I came to her unhealed and lacking childhood nurturance, love, protection, and guidance, I amazed myself at my aptitude for mothering. Unlike my sisters and other young girls, I never thought of marriage. I wanted four kids, but a husband never played into the fantasy. Yet there was this vast love inside of me that I wanted to pour into others. I adored dolls and Barbies and played with them longer than most girls, I suspect. However, the last one I received was for my twelfth birthday. It was a Cabbage Patch kid with brunette hair that grew, and she had a flowered dress and pink shoes. I kept her in perfect order and gave her to my daughter when she was little.

Growing up in a family of our size we didn't have an abundance of toys, and I learned to appreciate our parents' gifts. I took the best care of my dolls and never liked any of their shoes, clothing, or jewelry to go missing. My two older sisters had outgrown playing with dolls, so one of my favorite things to do was play dolls with my four younger sisters. We played church, which meant we pretended to be at a service, where they'd bring their imaginary husbands and children, and mimic how believers of our faith acted in church. They'd throw their hands in the air, weep, and loudly shout "Amen" and "Thank you, Jesus."

My focus was on my doll. I would tidy her clothing to make sure she was presentable and perfect. I'd smile at her and then snuggle her close, kissing her and telling her how much I loved her. Then I'd pretend she cried, and I'd rush off to the nursery and spank her for being bad. Children mimic what they see and believe. And when I look back at these memories, I can see how our childhoods unfold even in our playtime.

For years, when asked if there were any fond moments in my childhood, I would shrug and say "Not really" because I couldn't see past the painful memories and the home I had wanted to forget. Where my childhood house and memories had become my nightmare, the school had become my daughter's. She believed the hateful words of her peers. And a school year never went by without her being relentlessly bullied. They'd leave notes in her locker warning her not to go to the restroom, or they would beat her up. At lunch she sat alone and, in later years, in her car, where she'd find hateful notes on her windshield. It was a living nightmare for her to show up to school each day. As her parent, I felt utterly helpless. I tried to soothe her with statements like "It's not you," "We don't know what these kids face when they go home," "They probably have so much pain and self-loathing inside that they are using you as the target to release it."

But tell that to a child who's consumed with anxiety and can barely hold their head above water and expect them to be like, "Oh sure, Mom, that makes it all better. That takes the pain away." How can a child make sense of the heartache when all they can feel is *What is wrong with me?* She would ask, "Why doesn't anyone like me? Why can't I keep a friend? Why does this keep happening to me?" I didn't have the answers, and it frustrated me. I spent most of my rearing of her feeling handcuffed. I felt angry at the school, the parents, and the injustice children faced when trying to get an education.

In the earlier grades, teachers told me stories of how my daughter nurtured and cared for disabled classmates and spoke up for children mistreated by their peers. Later, they claimed my daughter suffered at the hands of bullies because she was sweet, talented, pretty, and liked by the boys, so other girls sought to tear her down.

In the middle of fifth grade, I received a message from her teacher informing me that my daughter needed to clean out her locker. First, I was confused over why she had to clean it out when it wasn't the end of the school year, and second why I had been asked to assist her. I arrived at the school and met her at her locker. When she opened it, a repulsive odor of spoiled food wafted out and I gathered why I'd been summoned, although no teacher met me to discuss the matter. I can only assume other students or teachers brought the condition of her locker to her homeroom teacher's attention. The chaos inside her locker came as no surprise because I had dealt with the same issue at home. Her room was always a mess, and she did not value her things or other people's, and she held no positive regard for herself.

One day the smell radiating from her closet caused me to investigate, and I was shocked to discover rotten lunches hidden behind items she'd taken from my son, myself, and my husband, but it was mainly my belongs she took. She'd taken my contacts, jewelry, sweaters too large for her petite, slim frame, and other odds and ends. The items served her no purpose, but she gathered them regardless. Dumbfounded and appalled by the odor, and the hoards of stuff she'd collected, I scolded her for taking my things and questioned her about why she felt the need to. And, furthermore, why wasn't she eating her lunches? She told me a girl at school had taunted her about being fat, so she refused to eat at school. I told her that the child didn't know what she was talking about because she was far from fat. I continued to reinforce how perfect she was just the way she was. However, it did little to dislodge her skewed perception of herself.

After that day, she stored the lunches in her locker to avoid my scolding and questioning. As I stood in front of her locker and realized it was still happening, frustration and helplessness erupted. I'm sure I reprimanded her on keeping it clean, which would only add to the shame and disconnect she felt with her body. However, my scolding did little to solve the issue because I then found the lunches in the garbage at home.

The bullying continued but the school was of no help, regardless of how many times I showed up and sent emails. Once they did go so far as bringing the parent of a child in to meet with my daughter, the principal, and myself, but it changed nothing. Teachers can only do so much. They can't be everywhere at once, and can't change what happens behind closed doors. The basis of a healthy foundation is security and stability, and it starts at home. Unfortunately, many kids don't receive what every child deserves. Some parents are incapable of love and meeting the needs of their children. Some lug around unhealed trauma and can't find the strength or desire to heal. Others set aside their own happiness so their kids never go without. As a result, their whole lives become about their children; which comes from love, but isn't healthy for the child or parent.

I'm aware of how, at times, my trauma hindered my parenting in profound ways. The challenges I faced in raising my daughter and my unhealed past only added to one of the most demanding jobs in the world. Throughout her life, she witnessed my stress and worry over her. She saw me break down and bury my face in my hands, crying because I wanted to help her but had no idea how.

Children are like sponges, so I can only imagine how she must've absorbed the blame for my anxiety and sadness, which would have elevated her own. I dreaded sending her to school each day and worried about what she would face. My life became filled with fear and anxiety over her well-being. Anger burrowed inside me, wanting justice for my child. I felt frustration toward the parents of the bullies, the school, and myself because I was her mother; I was supposed to protect her, and I felt helpless. I talked to friends and family, trying desperately to figure out how to help her, but came up empty-handed. I went to great lengths to encourage and support her, trying to communicate her worth. I enrolled her in extra activities such as swimming, music, and singing to give her an outlet. But it was to no avail. My daughter was deteriorating before me and had fallen into a deep depression.

I wanted to wrap her in bubble wrap and keep her close to

me to protect her. The situation was beyond my understanding, and I didn't have the tools to repair the damage done to her psyche. I didn't want her to grow up loathing or feeling disconnected from her body, or unsafe in her environment. I wanted so much better for her. She had witnessed my own disconnect and self-loathing of my body. It was like history was repeating itself in my daughter, and I blamed myself. I didn't know what to do or where to turn. I wanted her to get a proper education, but her grades continued to slip because she couldn't focus in class.

Heartsick, I couldn't allow her to endure the panic and fear of going to school. Although I wasn't a fan of homeschooling because of my own experience and how I'd slipped between the cracks, I felt I had no choice but to pull her from the public school system and homeschool her in her ninth grade. Thankfully, I worked for myself and could take her to the office with me. During that year, she informed me of the thoughts of suicide she'd struggled with, and the world crumbled around me. Feelings of shame and guilt overwhelmed me. How could I not have known it had gotten that bad? Why hadn't I been more observant? I had made a promise to protect my children, and I couldn't. I had failed her. I felt unfit as a parent, scared and alone. But then I felt guilty for feeling those emotions because it was her who was suffering.

After her revelation, fear gripped me like it never had before, and insomnia controlled my nights. Each little noise had me dashing to her room to check to see if she still breathed. The anxiety was so bad, I imagined each sound was her taking her last breath. Life became a living hell, and my mission to save her intensified.

For most of her life, my daughter sought acceptance from outside sources. She yearned to fit in. When she was ten, I required surgery and had to stay in the hospital for a few days, which would leave me unable to drive my children to school. Not having family around and not one to ask for help, I decided they would ride their bikes to school. Worried about someone taking them, I decided to get them each a cell phone, so if something was to happen, they could get in touch with their father or me. After the hospital stay, we neglected to take the phones away, and several months later, I received a phone bill for over $400 for my daughter's phone alone. I noticed incoming and outgoing calls to Rosewood, California. Alerted, I questioned my daughter, and she told me it was her friend, Dee. My stomach dropped, and I asked her if she sent pictures to this person. She said yes. I asked if she had told her where she lives. She said yes. She had gone as far as informing this person what school she attended. Despite warning my kids about the dangers of strangers, it'd gone in one ear and out the other with her. I called the number, and a raspy-voiced woman answered. I asked if she was Dee, and she said yes. I immediately hung up and went to the police. Nothing came from it, but I believe the person was grooming my daughter to kidnap her.

Later, when she was thirteen and permitted a phone again, I found information from a thirty-three-year-old man asking her and other young girls on an app if they were virgins, if they masturbated, and similar questions. I dropped to my knees with a guttural scream. Aware of the depths of my daughter's disconnect from herself and past experiences, I feared she was an easy target for pedophiles.

My daughter is twenty now, and recently while talking about what I would put in this book, she related how at one time, I wouldn't let her walk the dogs alone. I recall this time clearly. There was a lot of construction in our area, and I worried someone would take her. Not only had I been groomed to fear men and being raped, but my experiences with my daughter and her seeking fulfillment in others heightened my anxiety.

So many times, I struggled with my guidance in raising her. I wanted to do and say the right thing. I didn't want to damage my children.

For a short period, I got her to attend therapy, which she felt helped. She returned to school in the tenth grade because she was lonely and wanted to make friends.

Throughout her school years, she gravitated toward troubled kids, which only tightened my grip on her. She felt alone and blamed me for the friends that came and went. She started secretly dating a boy at thirteen, though my husband and I had set the rule that there would be no dating until the age of sixteen. I would say our rules were stricter than the average household. My son, an introvert, had no issues with the few rules we set: a curfew, and no parties or dating until sixteen; however, my daughter, a social butterfly, did. And she fought back about the injustice she felt. She craved freedom, but my fear over her disregard for herself tightened my iron grip. She snuck in and out of the house and lied about going to sleepovers and where else she was going.

In her midteens, she became defensive and often lashed out at her family. Her depression and anxiety intensified, and I urged her to go to therapy again, but she refused because she didn't want to be considered odd by her peers. Then I discovered that equine therapy was a thing. She fell in love with the horses, and the ranch became her escape.

Halfway through grade eleven, I was sitting in my living room when the door flew open. My daughter raced in after school and dropped to her knees. A look of anguish gripped her face. My heart seized, and I asked her what had happened.

"I can't do this," she wept. "Life isn't worth living like this."

I told her to come to sit with me, and she climbed onto my lap as she'd done as a little girl. I held her and soothed her with words of comfort as she told me what had happened at school. My heart broke for her. It felt like life or death at that moment. I would not lose my daughter.

I was already juggling three businesses; how could I possibly homeschool her again? And how in the world would I teach her algebra? I worried I'd be inadequate at teaching high school math because I had struggled with it myself in high school, but I wouldn't see her suffer another day in the school system.

"That's it," I said. "Tomorrow, we will go to school and get your things. You will never go back."

She breathed a sigh of relief and agreed she didn't want to return. One of her biggest fears was being isolated and alone, but she knew she could no longer take the bullying.

In hindsight, and despite striving not to, I understand I allowed my strict and conservative upbringing to seep into my own parenting. I was famous for saying, "Your few rules are nothing compared to the way I was raised." Or my husband's favorite: "You have more than I ever had." Later, when our daughter left home in a way that left our family devastated and reeling, I would cry and say to my husband, "She doesn't know what she has. I'd do anything to have a mom like she has."

As parents, we sometimes feel the need to compare what we did or didn't have in our childhood to what our children have. We work hard to give them all we never had, but blame and shame them for what we didn't receive with such statements. Why should our children bear the burden of the disadvantaged feelings conditioned into us? What children need above all the luxuries we can offer is love, protection, and guidance. It will serve them in life, more than all the gifts we could possibly give them. Gifts come and go and become a distant memory, but the time you put into raising healthy and supported children is a gift like no other. Your children will never forget how you made them feel.

I am aware of the restrictions I put on my daughter and how circumstances with her caused me to parent her differently than my son. Although I understood that all children are unique and each requires attention and guidance tailored to their particular needs, I acknowledge that, at points in my daughter's life, my conditioning added more harm than good. Too often, I parented from the viewpoint of my inner child, where fear and anxiety took form. The unhealed little girl inside me trilled to my daughter's pain, often screaming, "Me too. Hey, over here! I know what it feels like. I've been there. I bear the marks. I'll protect you. I will save you from pain." So, guided by the pain and fear of my inner child, I didn't trust that my adult self had the consciousness or intelligence to be what my daughter needed.

For the most part, I applaud myself for the mother I was, despite the childhood I had. Other times, I flounder in regret and blame over ways I believed I had failed my daughter. However, I am grateful that my awareness of the absence of healthy parenting in my life helped me to be a better mother than my children would've gotten if I hadn't spent my life seeking healing.

Raising my daughter came with its challenges, and I learned my share of lessons in the experience. The effects of bullying can last a lifetime, and no child should ever have to endure what she went through. School should be a safe place for children to receive an education. Unfortunately, there isn't enough being done in schools to stop bullying. Awareness of the issue can't be on a surface level, where posters are slapped up on school walls, stating a No Tolerance for Bullying policy that isn't enforced.

One glance at social media will reveal the scope of trolling, hate speech, racism, and belittling of others by adults who deem others different and less than. They inflict their self-loathing and disconnect of themselves on others. These people are bullies and create the bullies in the world's playground. But, unfortunately, they have their part to play in raising the next generation.

Healed parents raise healthy children who will create a better tomorrow for all of us. It doesn't mean our children won't have bumps in the road and walk their own journey. They will and should. Our view of the future and theirs will be different, as it should be. We are all individuals.

Humanity has a responsibility to make our world a better place, and our most important role in life is to heal ourselves, and by doing so, we administer the change the world needs. Love always wins, and that love starts within us.

Stepping-Stone Exercises

Too often, we get in our own way by carrying our story and reliving it through a place of hurt and fear, which does us a disservice. If we constantly have flashbacks to our childhood, which keep us stuck, we can't move on. Forgiving our wrongdoers doesn't mean what they did to us was okay. It is us claiming our personal power. It's saying they did this, but I am in control of my life, body, mind, and spirit. Forgiveness releases us from their grip.

Take a moment to think back to a time when you felt unprotected. How did that situation impact you? Have you carried hate and anger in your heart for the ones involved? Perhaps you bore the shame, guilt, or responsibility for something that wasn't your fault. Evaluate the situation in its entirety with an open mind and a desire to heal and release. Maybe there is an incident where you put yourself in danger and have spent a lifetime beating yourself up over it. You deserve to be free of the burden you have placed on yourself. The self-inflicted punishment ends today! Award compassion and forgiveness to yourself. We are all human, and we make mistakes.

Affirmation

I am a light in the world. Each day I rise and smile at another; I spread love and kindness. I am the creator of my words and actions, and I choose ones that positively impact others. I award myself the same kindness, and in doing so, I claim my personal power. I deserve to thrive and live a beautiful life.

12–BODY SHAME

"We live in a world where most people still subscribe to the belief that shame is a good tool for keeping people in line. Not only is this wrong, but it's dangerous. Shame is highly correlated with addiction, violence, aggression, depression, eating disorders, and bullying." ~ **Brené Brown**

Toxic shame and body dissociation set in by the time puberty struck at twelve years old. As my body began to change I experienced confusion, fear, and revulsion over what was happening. I wanted to go to my mother, but I didn't want to get into trouble and kept it a secret. Then my first menstruation hit, and the sight of blood on my underwear scared me and filled me with shame. I hid my underwear under my mattress instead of putting them in the wash because I was terrified of my family knowing my body's revolting behaviors. My younger sisters ended up finding the soiled underwear. They raced through the house, broadcasting my humiliation for all to see, which embarrassed me for hiding the garments in the first place and because my body was doing something wrong.

Throughout our teen years, my mother never permitted us to shave our legs or other body parts. Later in life my father was shocked that she'd never allowed it. When it came to matters of female anatomy, he left the education to my mother. Because all we wore were dresses or skirts, I'd never go bare-legged, and wore tights or pantyhose all year round because I didn't want others to see my unshaved legs. Once, I was permitted to spend the night at the house of a girl from our church and we had to share a twin bed. As we prepared for bed, her in the bathroom and me in her room, my nerves roiled as I contemplated how I would hide my hairy legs from her. In the end, I chose to wear my pantyhose under my nightgown. The girl noticed and asked why I was wearing them to bed, and I quickly made an excuse before changing the subject.

Although Mom had birthed a houseful of girls, she never educated us on our anatomy. I didn't know how babies were created and until I was eighteen years old; I thought if I lay next to a man on a bed, I would get pregnant. I hadn't the slightest clue where babies came from. I remember finding a book under the couch with black and white diagrams of a woman pushing out a baby, and this is how I learned babies came out from a woman's lower region. Not knowing anything about male or female anatomy, I thought babies came out the urethral opening. Repulsed, I threw the book back under the couch, where I can only assume my mother had hidden it.

My parents requested I be removed from sex education class, and the walk of shame from my seat until I could breathe again outside the room and beyond the peering eyes of my classmates felt like death. Each year that sex education was taught, I sat in the library until the class was over. Not only did my parents' decision to remove us from the class alienate me from my peers, which I was already sensitive to because I was different, but it neglected to educate me on a critical subject concerning a young woman's development.

My mother claims she was too embarrassed to talk about such matters. So for years I let it rest at that, because I recalled how I'd never witnessed my parents ever show affection toward each other. But obviously they had some sort of physical connection, because—well, they had seven kids. And when I was around sixteen or so, I went to open the front door and got a quick look at my mom standing within the open door of my dad's truck before my oldest sister almost knocked me over in her hurry to shut the door. I stepped back and regarded her in shock and confusion.

"You can't go out there," she said.

"Why?" I scowled at her.

"Because they're kissing!"

Her desperation to prevent me from seeing such a sight speaks to the rareness of our parents showing affection. However, I can attest that as much as I never observed love between them, I don't recollect them fighting or arguing, aside from the odd fuss over her wasting money. My mother says it was because of embarrassment on her side that they never showed affection in public and that my dad tried.

Until grade five, I had been permitted to play sports and had developed a love for basketball, but to take physical education, you had to wear proper attire. So my mom fashioned me a pair of knee-length, white-and-pink pinstripe skorts. Pants were viewed as men's apparel, so we wore long dresses or skirts so, in the skort, I felt awkward and naked. But as my body started to develop, I was no longer permitted to take gym. Instead, I had to sit on the bleachers or the stage while my peers took part. I yearned to play and felt isolated, envious, ashamed, and embarrassed when my classmates sent looks of pity or mockery my way. Throughout junior high and high school, Physical Education was my worst subject. I failed the class in high school because I didn't understand the games or rules when it came to the written test. The theory behind my father's refusal to allow us to do sports was that our breasts would bounce and draw the attention of men.

By withholding education about the basic biology of the body, I was kept in the dark when it came to the essential, fundamental understandings that would have aided me in my development from a child to a woman. If my mother had provided the necessary information, it would've equipped me for life and eased the growing disgust for a body I believed was defective because it was doing things I didn't understand. Instead, my mother deliberately withheld any knowledge of bodily functions and how they should or shouldn't look. The extremes she'd go to were revealed in the Sears catalog. I loved the *Wish Book* and looked forward to the release each year. When I got my turn with the catalog, I savored each page, dreaming of owning all the Barbies and Cabbage Patch Kids. It was expected you'd see all the models' bodies blacked out when you got to the women's and men's underwear sections. My mom used a black marker and scribbled out the nakedness, leaving only the models' heads. My parents did the same with movies. It was normal for the picture to disappear, replaced with black and gray fuzziness, and several moments passed before the picture would return. As an adult, I rewatched these Bible and other movies of my youth that are tame in comparison to today's films and realized the kissing and PG-rated intimacy scenes had been recorded over.

If I hadn't married a patient, kind man, who had been raised in a different home environment with his own trauma, but with the understanding of the dogma of our youth, I wonder what struggles other relationships would have brought. I would've eventually learned what I needed to understand my development during my formative years, but at what cost?

A funny story of my naivete from when I was around eighteen: I sat with my best and only friend at the time in my family's van in the yard, the only place we could be away from the pestering of my little sisters. I sat in the driver's seat and she sat in the passenger seat. She told me I had to take my clothes off to have sex.

My head snapped around, and I gawked at her in horror. "What? That is disgusting. I'm never doing that."

Sadly, it's true that my naivete went that deep.

I was sixteen or seventeen the first time I tried on a pair of pants. Katie convinced me, on one of the rare occasions that I was allowed to spend the night at her house, to try on pants and let her do my makeup. I recall the panic I felt as I quickly shook my head.

"No, I would get in trouble."

"They will never know. It's not a big deal," she said. "Let's just see what you would look like."

Out of curiosity and a desire to please her, I allowed her to weave her magic. She applied a full face of makeup and finished with a wine-colored lipstick, her favorite shade at the time. I sensed her delight and eagerness to defy my parents and liberate me. She didn't know the extent of what would happen to me if they found out. Heart racing and palms sweating, I squirmed as I waited for her to finish.

Katie stepped back and admired her work before removing a pair of black jeans from her closet. She tossed them at me. "Here, put these on."

I shook my head. "I can't." Fear and shame melded. I had

already sinned when I allowed her to do my makeup. God would surely punish me now. But, in all honesty, it was the wrath of my dad and the beating I would get that scared me most—and the shame and disappointment my parents would unleash.

"Come on. They will never know," she reiterated.

"I don't know." My hesitation continued, but upon further urging I gave in and slipped the jeans on beneath my dress. The tightness of the fabric felt restrictive in comparison to my usual oversized clothing that hid my curves.

After I buttoned the jeans, I pulled on the cream, long-sleeved T-shirt she held out.

"Look!" she said, pointing at the mirror.

Panic thrummed as I lifted my eyes to regard myself. I gulped at the reflection staring back at me. I recall thinking I looked weird and never liked the makeup, but it was my body that I focused on. Although I was slim and probably about a size eight or ten (I never knew my size, as most of my clothes were made for me), I felt thick and hated my reflection. I appraised Katie and how, in my recollection, the jeans hadn't clung to her body as tightly as they did mine. Then, internally, I criticized her. She only wanted to defy my parents. My parents had been right; she was a bad influence. She wanted to cause me harm and discourse with my parents. I couldn't trust her.

When she suggested we get the new video camera my grandfather had purchased, my body tensed. "Have you lost your mind?" I cried. "What if my parents ever saw it?"

"They won't," she assured me.

Somehow, she persuaded me to allow her to, and I had almost forgotten about the incident until six months to a year later, when my mother brought us to visit my grandfather. We all sat in the living room, and my grandfather decided to show my mother something on the home videos he had taped. He asked Katie to get the video camera. At his mention, I remembered that day in her room, and my stomach knotted. As the home video played, I waited anxiously, imagining my end. And then, there it was. My secret broadcasted across the screen for all to see, and my heart stopped. Fear coursed through my veins. I don't know how it happened, but to my relief, my mother had turned her head at that moment, or perhaps didn't recognize me. In charge of the video recorder, Katie quickly fast-forwarded the evidence, and I wanted to strangle her for playing with my life.

My psyche had been at war with my body from early on in adolescence. I can trace conditioned self-belief to many factors in my youth, from my father's fear that his daughters would become "fallen women" like his sisters (which meant they were divorced, some multiple times) and the need for control that dominated his parenting. His concern that we'd become fallen women hung over us like a storm cloud I couldn't escape. Often it felt like I was being punished for something I'd never done. I could never be enough in his eyes because of his incessantly comparing us to his sisters.

Although I never spoke my fears to my daughter, in parenting her, I too inwardly compared her to other family members. Throughout her school years, she learned to manipulate to get what she wanted and lied to get out of trouble and later, when she took items, sometimes money, from my husband and I. All characteristics I detested, and as I saw them unfold in her I feared what kind of life she would lead with these behaviors.

My father gave up his role as pastor when I was in my early teens, and we started attending a church an hour away. At this new church, women were not to show their legs or feet because it could cause "a brother" to fall. I remember thinking men were weak and pathetic if something as minuscule as feet or a glimpse of a women's legs would make them forgo their beliefs and dedication to a Christian path. However, these teachings made me feel I'd be responsible if a man turned from God because I had lured him with my body, which intensified my issues with body shame and belief in my inadequacy.

∾

In dissecting my issues with body shame and in hopes of helping others who have also struggled with loving their bodies, I won't hold back. Instead, I'll lay it all out there, revealing things about myself that I, at one time, considered humiliating and embarrassing.

As earlier mentioned, I am a big-boned, curvy girl, and it has taken me years to embrace my body and appreciate the reflection I see in the mirror. As a result, I've gone to extreme measures in hopes of securing freedom from the weight.

Off and on for two decades, I carried around a shield of fat, and in pursuing my first issues with negative body image and a toxic relationship with food, I could trace it back to childhood.

Dad would make remarks about my shape when I was a teenager and say I was built like a farmer's wife. Which was a stereotype on his part because they come in many sizes. Other times, he would try to pinch the fat on me and tell me I needed to get out walking with my mom, who continues to battle with weight. As a result, I became obsessed with exercise, skipping meals, and belittling myself. When I reflect on pictures of myself in my teenage years, I was indeed broad-shouldered and tall, but I was thin; however, at the time, I thought I was huge.

Siblings being siblings, my sisters gave me the nickname "Bull Moose." My father's nicknames for me were "Dumper," or "Dumpie," and "Hom-I-Lean." I don't believe any of them did it out of malice.

As a teen, I often looked at my inner thighs and stomach and pinched at the minimal bits of flesh and imagined taking a knife and sawing away the shame. In my mind, I saw a fat girl, and what may have been five pounds reflected as thirty to fifty. My knowledge of weight and fixation on a number on the scale would take hold in my midteens. I recall going for a dress fitting with a lady at our church, and she took my measurements and said, "I would never have guessed you were that big." Also, around this time, I stepped on the scale for the first time in my recollection. When the daunting number of 171 glared back at me, profound shame blanketed me. I don't know why that number affected me so harshly, or how I concluded it was an alarming number, but it shook me. That weight is my ideal weight.

The number on the scale holds only a fraction of the truth in the reality of your situation, and a prime example of why we can't compare our clothing size and bodies to others is my oldest sister and me. In our teenage years, she weighed fifty pounds less than me. Often, when she left for school (a different one than mine), I would go to her closet, sneak her clothes, wear them for the day, and return them to the hanger before she returned home.

These incidents, along with several others, were the origin of my self-loathing and negative self-talk. Only by peeling back each painful layer have I discovered the force behind my weight issues and that my unhealthy relationship with food came from a place of lack. A child requires nurturance, guidance, and protection, which Kelly McDaniel lays out beautifully in her book *Mother Hunger*. Unfortunately, these fundamentals were withheld from me as a child, and somewhere along the way, I learned food brought comfort, regardless of how fleeting it may be.

I remember there never being enough food in our house. So when our guests were done with their meals, we sometimes had the leftovers. I remember serving them five-course meals and wishing I could have the abundance they received. At 4:00 a.m., we older girls rose to help prepare breakfast for the guests before school. I recall standing over the griddle, tending the bacon as it sizzled and popped, and savoring the thought of what it would taste like, but knowing it was off-limits. Instead, we prepared the table and laid out stacks of fluffy pancakes, scrambled eggs, bacon, syrup, orange juice, and coffee, and stood back, waiting to tend to the needs of my father and the guests.

Dad was a king in our house. And he indulged like one too, never seeming to care that his children did not. When Mom would make homemade bread and pies, my dad would tell us not to touch them before disappearing into his room with a whole pie and a fork. When he purchased a watermelon, he cut out the heart for himself and gave us the rinds and what pink flesh was left. I didn't have the luxury of a snack because food too was limited, like everything in my adolescence.

Once I opened a new bottle of pickles, and my father came unglued, saying, "As long as you're in this house, don't you ever open anything without my permission."

I resolved I wasn't good enough to have the luxuries destined for others.

An atmosphere of servitude reigned supreme in our house. If you walked into my parents' room without permission, you were assigned the task of rubbing his feet. We jumped and scurried at the mere sound of his voice.

∽

For his business, my father purchased outdated donuts, bread, and apples to use as bait to lure in the animals. The food was kept in an old barn, with buckets of old grease and molasses for the bears. Often, my sisters and I would dig through the crates for food that hadn't mildewed. I dreaded going into the barn because it smelled, and mice are my nemesis.

Despite the theme of scarcity in our lives, as my dad did better financially in my later teen years, my parents took us once or twice a year to a McDonald's drive-thru, where they ordered seven Happy Meals for us girls. I remember the nonstop train of boxes as they passed from hand to hand to the back of the van. The nearest McDonald's was across the US border, which became an adventure of sorts and gave me a sense of grandeur. On another occasion, I recall going to Pizza Hut and dining in. The staff placed tables together in the middle of the restaurant to accommodate us. Happy faces, chatter, and laughter permeated the restaurant from the patrons. And at our table, for the moment, the accustomed tension and fear dissipated as my parents and us girls escaped into euphoria.

Sometimes my parents went for dinner by themselves and would bring home leftovers, and on occasion, they let us have them. Of course you only got a bite, with all the children, but regardless, it was delectable. Other times Mom would go into the village and purchase us each a sucker, or they would buy a bag of chips and a two-liter bottle of soda. We older girls would measure the servings evenly because we didn't want to miss out on our share. In time, I came to associate food with happiness, love, and comfort, and a way of grounding myself.

The closest town to our house had few restaurants, but KFC had opened, and one day while waiting in the van for my mother,

I eyed the signage in the window featuring the Big Crunch sandwich. This day, I had a few dollars, and after some contemplation, I purchased the sandwich and returned to the car with an urgency to devour it before my mother got back.

Early on, I harbored feelings over what I deemed gluttonous behaviors in my mother. I considered her lazy, unfit, and at times unintelligent because simple common sense often escaped her. As a result, I spent most of my life trying to be anyone but her, and although we are entirely different people, we shared the connection to food, our desire to numb the pain, and our painful childhoods.

Happy memories in my childhood revolved around food. One year that we celebrated Christmas, my dad purchased mixed nuts with the shells on, peach juice boxes that we ate like sorbet because they were frozen, grapes, and a box of bananas. We prepared a Christmas dinner with all the fixings and sat at the table.

Also, we received gifts, and when my friend called to ask what I had gotten, I was excited to have something to tell her. I told her about the watch and other items I received before telling her about the food. This was also the year Dad rented movies.

After high school, I started to gain weight when I became a live-in nanny for a single mom in the Canadian Forces. She agreed to pay me $200 a month and provide lodging and food. I was to care for her one-year-old and six-year-old while she was at work. But soon it became clear that she was abusing her access to me, and I took on a greater workload than what we had agreed on. On her days off, which included weekends, her children wandered down to the unfinished basement of the PMQ where I slept and climbed into my bed for morning cuddles while their mother slept in.

I soon understood that the men who filtered in and out of the PMQ mattered more to her than her children. And I developed a fierce protectiveness for the children. I did my best to provide love and kindness—maybe because I was more mature, I had more patience with them than I'd had when caring for my little sisters.

The home had one bathroom and three upstairs bedrooms. Every time she had sex, I was alerted because her dramatics and the thumping of the bed in her second-floor bedroom could be heard through the vents in my basement room. This was my first exposure to sex. The whole ordeal sounded awful and violent, and my concerns often turned to the children because their rooms were next to hers. Other times, I had to go to the bathroom and paused halfway up the stairs at the wailing, thumping, and splashing of water coming from behind the closed door. I developed an appreciation for the shielded intimacy between my parents.

During my stay with the family I came down with the flu, and the woman suggested I could sleep in her bed to be closer to the bathroom. At first I didn't want any part of it because whatever happened inside that bedroom terrified the life out of me, but eventually the need to be closer to the bathroom became overwhelming and I gave in. I was in for an awakening when I noticed a video titled *The Last Blonde* near the VCR and popped it in. I figured the movie would be like *The Last Unicorn*. (Yes, I was that naïve.) Well, it wasn't, and within a few seconds I quickly received my sexual education. My new awareness of what unfolded in the room between her and her partners made me want to be anywhere but in that bed. With this enlightenment, I decided what happened during sex was painful and to be avoided.

It was common to see soldiers coming down the stairs in the morning on my way up to the washroom. I'd hold my breath and squeeze by them to rush up the stairs and find safety behind the bathroom's locked door. Upon my return to the main floor the soldier would be gone, and I'd breathe a sigh of relief. I dreaded when she hosted parties. Not accustomed to people drinking, I hid in my room, listening to the drunken laughter and hooting coming from above. Once an intoxicated soldier showed up in my room, and all my mother's warnings flashed through my mind. Thankfully, after stumbling around and incoherently blabbering, he left and wandered back upstairs.

The isolation and lack of education regarding the outside world had me spinning with fear and anxiety. I'd thrown myself into a foreign environment where my conditioned belief was that every person who walked in and out of the home was a sinner and evil. I yearned for safety, and for the year and a bit that I lived there, I never found it. My love for the children kept me there longer than I should have stayed. My income barely paid for my phone, personal hygiene items, and clothing, but I ensured I'd have enough money to have fast food or pizza once or twice a month. I looked forward to payday because food brought comfort. At her house, food was more accessible. With her job as an army cook, she often brought home outdated items from the kitchen.

Then, one day after I'd been with the family for almost a year, she sat me down and told me what I could and couldn't eat. I recall feeling embarrassed and wondered if I had overeaten, and my sense of unworthiness surfaced. Again, food came with the restrictions I had experienced at home. Also, during that conversation, she informed me that with the $200 a month she paid me, I should be saving money to buy a car. I frowned at her while contemplating how she expected me to save for a car, pay insurance, and still cover personal needs. Although I didn't hold a basic understanding of the natural world, I knew I needed to make more money, and it wouldn't happen with her because, by then, she'd started abusing my naivety and had me watching her children around the clock for the same pay rate.

At twenty, I married my husband of now twenty-three years, and we had two children by the time I turned twenty-three. At twenty-five, I suffered my first panic attack, and the doctor put me on medication that I stayed on for ten years. Over that time, I gained seventy pounds. My food association turned to self-loathing, disgust, and shame as my weight crept up. I tried the newest fad diets that promised to be the cure to my weight issue. I starved myself and worked out excessively. My weight fluctuated up and down. I'd lose thirty to fifty pounds and then gain it all back and then some. I came to hate every inch of my body.

I dreaded going shopping because the clothes never fit right, and I had to face the truth in the mirror. I was obese, food dominated me, and I felt helpless and defeated by life. I'd stand there and belittle myself, telling myself I was weak and a failure. "Why can't you just stop!" I'd scream at my reflection. I noted the pain in my eyes and dropped my head in shame. I felt like a prisoner in the fat suit that confined the healthy, slimmer version inside me, begging to step into the light. I punished myself horribly for the shame I bore over my weight.

One day I went shopping with my daughter, who was two or three at the time, and she stood in front of the mirror and patted her tummy, saying, "I fat." My heart broke, and I cried as I looked at her happily repeating the statement I had said over and over aloud, then I rebuked myself for the poor example I had become for her. Although I tried to be more mindful of what I said aloud, my self-loathing never ceased.

A few days before my father died, I remember sitting in my living room with my youngest sister and telling her, "If it wasn't for the weight, I would be perfectly happy." The truth was, I had a beautiful life. I had a great marriage and two exceptional children, and we were all healthy. I owned a gorgeous home, had fancy cars, traveled the world, owned my own businesses, and possessed all the luxuries one could want. If I could just escape the fat suit, everything would be great, I told myself.

Several months after my father died, I'd reached my highest weight and was miserable.

A friend had returned from having weight surgery, which she'd kept secret. As she miraculously started shedding weight, I inquired, and she told me she'd gone to Mexico and underwent gastric sleeve surgery. I thought she was reckless to go to Mexico for surgery, and alone at that. However, as I watched her progress, I was amazed and yearned to find the same freedom from the shame I carried. I called my husband, crying and telling him I just needed to be free. "I can't live like this," I wept into the phone. He had witnessed my endless diets, hours at the gym, and self-loathing. He loved me at my thinnest and my heaviest, and supported my choice to have the surgery. Another friend and I went to Mexico and both had the surgery, and while my friends dropped quickly to their goal weight, I didn't. I spent two to three years drinking protein shakes, eating Greek yogurt, shrimp, chicken, and vegetables. I stayed religiously strict with the food plan the doctor had laid out for me while my friends ate cookies, McDonald's, and drank sugar-laced lattes. I abused myself by comparing myself to them. "I'm doing everything I'm supposed to. Why isn't my weight dropping like theirs did," I moaned to my husband and family. Although I was losing weight and had dropped five to six dress sizes, I still saw a fat girl in the mirror.

Over the following years, I lost 120 pounds, had skin removal surgery, and acquired the body of my dreams. I stuck to my eating plan, and my unhealthy detours with food turned to working out for a minimum of four hours a day. Then I started a new business, and to get it off the ground, I worked sixteen- to eighteen-hour days. I became stressed and burned out. I couldn't balance everything. We ate out more because I didn't have the energy to cook. I made healthy food choices about 60 to 70 percent of the time. My extensive workouts fell by the wayside, replaced with a daily walk. Sugary and high-fat foods made me experience flu-like symptoms, so they weren't my usual choice to numb the pain. Fine dining and hanging with friends gave me the adventure and happiness I'd come to connect with food.

Before I took on the new business, I hosted lavish dinner parties to spoil my friends and family two or three times a year. Each event required one to two months of planning. First I met with my cake designer to have a beautiful art piece as a focal point. Then I spent weeks planning the menu, fresh flowers, games, and prizes. I loved to see the joy and happiness on my guest's faces, and it was my way of showing them love. I wanted them to feel special, and I sought to create experiences and memories with them.

All that went by the wayside, as did my time for friends and family outside my kids and husband. I numbed the stress and fatigue with food and stopped prioritizing my health as my fear of failure and lack of money took precedence. As a result, my weight started to climb, and I felt defeated. I suffered from chronic back and neck pain, adrenal gland fatigue, hormone imbalance, and migraines. It had become intolerable, to the point where I sat on the couch one day and tears of helpless overtook me as I said words similar to what my daughter had said several years before: "Life isn't worth living like this. I can't handle the pain."

I've given my all to my family and friends. My time and my money. I was a fixer and a people pleaser. I wanted everyone to be happy, and I wanted happiness for myself, but deep down, I didn't believe I deserved it and often wallowed in guilt for the beautiful life I had created. I spent too much time trying to prove my worth.

I've been an all-or-nothing girl. With this new business, I wanted to prove to others and my husband that I didn't need a man to define me. I also wanted to show my daughter she could do anything she wanted and didn't need a man to do it. Please don't misread my intention here. I believe in the value of all men, women, and children, but I believe in the value of a woman's independence too.

This new business was the first time I had done something I was genuinely passionate about. But with the fear of deficiency and my need to prove myself, I had put my vision of health, wellness, and self-love on the back burner. My skewed idea of being a superwoman crippled me. My business was on the way to success but I had gained some weight back in the process. I berated myself for the large amount I'd spent on my body. My failure stared back at me in the mirror. I had been so focused on my new business, and the ones I had with my husband, that I had abandoned myself. My god, what would people think? They would know I'm a failure. What would they say behind my back? Did they laugh and ridicule me? The shame and disheartenment became unbearable.

Stepping-Stone Exercises

Imagine your inner child in all their innocence and beauty. Now, pull this precious child close and wrap the adult you's arm around their shoulder. You are the protector, the nurturer, and the one who will guide your inner child to wholeness. All you never received in your childhood, you will give now.

What does your inner child long for? Is it to be free? Do you yearn for acceptance? Love? Protection? What is it?

Close your eyes, and I want you to envision the most precious child in your life. Look how the light reflects off their hair. Notice the soft glow of their cheeks and the perfect innocence encompassing them. Now, in your mind, tell that child, "You aren't enough. You aren't smart. You will never amount to anything." It's difficult, isn't it?

Now, tell this precious little person the words you always wanted to hear: "You are loved. You are perfect, just the way you are." Say it with gusto! Let your heart expand with the belief, and let the love radiate through you. You are lovable right now. You are pretty enough right now. As you continue to nurture your inner child you will come to believe these words, and you will be surprised how fast you can uproot outdated beliefs and step into your power. An appreciation for yourself and all the amazing qualities you possess will take form. The world will come alive in ways you've never experienced before.

During the healing of my inner child, I felt the urge to bundle up on a -20° Celsius day and go outside. I walked to the middle of my backyard and lay on the ground and peered up at the sky before proceeding to make snow angels. My dogs bounced with excitement around me, licking my face and carrying on. I laughed and swept my arms and legs faster as I gave in to my inner child's desire to be silly and free. I've never forgotten the rush of euphoria that came over me. Again, something so simple freed a part of me that had been locked away.

In his book, *The Untethered Soul*, Michael Singer speaks of the roommate, and during my reading of his work, I realized my roommate was negative and critical. Through his work, I learned to set an intention when I open my eyes each morning to not be guided by the roommate in my head, and to watch and listen to my own inner critic.

My father used to bemoan lyrics that went like, "Lonely days, and lonely nights, filled with despair. No one to long for, no one to care." For decades, I chanted the same tune, and it wasn't until I discovered the impact of the language we speak to ourselves and our thoughts that I was astonished at the negativity I daily told myself. Although I had always believed in the power of words, this song bypassed my radar.

13–THE FISHBOWL

"Perfectionism is a self-destructive and addictive belief
system that fuels this primary thought: If I look perfect, and
do everything perfectly, I can avoid or minimize the painful
feelings of shame, judgment, and blame." ~ **Brené Brown**

The pressure we put on ourselves to be perfect is maddening. Societal conditioning influences men to be masculine and strong and teaches our young boys to avoid displaying emotions. From a tender age, they learn to stifle their feelings and pursue superhero status. Since the dawn of time, men have been considered the providers and the protectors. They are trained to sense the honor in those tasks, but with it comes a substantial burden that robs them of their ability to just be human.

My husband is a fantastic spouse and father. Throughout his life, he has been driven by the need to provide for his family above all. I've watched him suppress his own desires and dreams to the point where he didn't know what made him happy. He worked morning to night and would come home and fall into bed. "No play, all work" became his motto. Often I would say to him, "You go through life with your ass in the air and head down. Like your only purpose is to work." He came from a place of privation, but he also chased the vision of being the stand-up guy who never let others down and believed his sole purpose was providing for and protecting our family. After years of fighting to fill the superhero uniform, he too became burnt out. The gleam in his blue-green eyes faded and he simply existed, and nothing more. The emptiness in his eyes scared me because he had always been a passionate person, but it was as though he'd become dead inside. If I asked him what lit him up, he'd say, "Nothing anymore." I'd come back with a reworded question. "Well, what makes you happy?" His gaze would drift off, and I observed his pondering. "I honestly don't know anymore," he finally replied. The desire to simplify our lives took root through these years, with me being the driving force. I wanted my husband back. I wanted to see the sparkle return to his eyes. As I had tried with my daughter, I endeavored to save him and return him to wholeness while the little girl locked inside of me begged for the same dedication. Although I considered myself under construction, I had embraced my passions. Yet I still wasn't happy, because I too chased the fantasy of perfection.

Women have a similar, yet different, ladder to climb in their efforts to attain perfection. The media brainwashes our young girls into believing perfection comes with beauty and a specific body shape. Your shade of skin is too light or too dark. You can't be too slim, too curvy, or too fat. Barbie and Ken have been portrayed as the ideal bodies for men and women. Many women worship the sun in hopes of achieving the perfect glow. I too was one of these women. My idea was that tanned fat looked better than white fat. We consistently compare ourselves to the media's idea of beauty. It's impossible to appreciate and love yourself when you are chasing other peoples' conceptions. You strip yourself of the ability to be authentically you.

We also had to push to prove our worth in a society considered a man's world. The need to balance the masculine energy with the feminine is critical going forward, but I won't get into the politics of that battle.

Instead, I return to the dynamic push for body positivity. However, like several movements taking hold globally, change won't fully produce the benefits until generational conditioning has faded. Unfortunately, with mental illness being taboo until the last few decades, we have unhealed parents, grandparents, caregivers, teachers, and influencers guiding and influencing the next generations. We can achieve a better world by sealing our lips, opening our ears, and observing; in doing so, we become aware on a deeper level. This change will make a positive difference in a world overflowing with hate, misguidance, and ancestral and generational trauma.

∽

As a child, I heard stories of how, after I started favoring my left hand, my dad would tie it behind me as I sat in the highchair and force me to use my right. His conditioned belief was that it was a right-handed world, and I would suffer as a left-handed person. He told me there were more opportunities for right-handed people. The same notion arose in him when my then fifteen-month-old daughter also favored her left hand.

In first grade, my teacher provided left-handed scissors to another girl and me because she believed they'd work better for us. Unfortunately, the scissors didn't work at all. They were horrible. I learned I could cut better by reversing a regular pair of scissors. The following year, my second-grade teacher read an article stating that, historically, left-handed people were considered evil. The article sealed the belief in me. Dad had been right.

I couldn't learn to play the guitar. I would have a hard time in life. But I also wondered why the world hadn't made a place for me.

∽

The grooming for perfectionism set the stage for us girls. "You are to be seen and not heard" was an oft-repeated statement. Image was everything with my parents. And what others thought held far too much influence. Giving weight to what others think and trying to please everyone is like a death sentence. You will never make others happy. Yet, I did it all and jumped through hoops to earn my parents' approval until it dawned on me that, unless I walked in their shadows, I would never be enough for them. I'd never be accepted, and I had to learn to become okay with that. It's natural for children to seek their parents' approval, but if you chase what makes others happy and seek acceptance outside of yourself, you will never be satisfied. Your acceptance of yourself is all that matters.

As my father rose in position in the religion and became known, the pressure from my parents to be perfect heightened. They informed us we had to be perfect because everyone watched, and our behavior would bring reproach to my father. Or they'd say, "It's like you're in a fishbowl, and the whole world is watching."

Those statements not only put me on edge about messing up, but reinforced an already acquired perception that my thoughts and feelings were not valid. I could never let down my guard. It instilled tension and leeriness toward those around me. If I didn't say the right thing or behave appropriately, adults would report me. I would be punished and disappoint my family. The way I clenched my jaw to ground myself and find some sort of control over myself, I've witnessed in several of my siblings.

From the rigid set of my jaw, the pain would radiate from my teeth as I braced to ward off an impending attack. I was conditioned to believe the waters outside the fishbowl were "dark and dangerous" and sharks lurked, seeking to devour me. I learned to dissociate from my mind, emotions, and body.

Being raised with this mentality is disempowering and has a significant impact on the foundation on which you stand. On the one hand, I stumbled through life like a toddler first finding their legs and with so much uncertainty. On the other, like a stoic commander, I needed to control myself and my environment to feel safe and good enough. It oppresses and strips you of your own sense of right and wrong. It significantly shaped my life.

My parents bought in hard to the religion. They controlled every aspect of my life. Because I have always been a deep thinker, it caused more conflict with my parents when I was in my late teens. If you had a mind of your own, it was dismissed as not of God and a worldly attitude sneaking in. All questions about how teachings didn't line up were rebuked. You were taught not to think for yourself or expand your mind. You were told how to think and feel, and to quell the need to question anything. I had to be perfect, and a woman with too many questions about wisdom best left to a man was silenced.

As an adult, I never allowed myself to make mistakes, and if I did, I rebuked myself forever and a day. But, of course, others around me could mess up, and I'd offer an abundance of grace and compassion and reassure them it was no big deal. We were humans, and humans make mistakes, I'd say. All while never extending myself the same grace and mercy.

Perfection doesn't mean you can't require excellence. It simply means you give yourself permission to be human. To some degree, we are all flawed.

Affirmation

I don't need to be perfect.
Perfectionism is an illusion I no
longer seek to achieve. I love myself
exactly the way I am. I am enough;
right here, right now. I live a life of
my making and on my terms.
No goal is too big for me.
I achieve what feels right to me.

14–VISIBLE

"We know through painful experience that freedom is never voluntarily given by the oppressor; it must be demanded by the oppressed." ~ **Martin Luther King Jr.**

A sense of adventure arose when my oldest sister, who had barely gotten her license, drove Dad's old blue single-cab pickup over the pothole-riddled road to the woods to gather wood. I forwent sitting inside and rode on the heaping pile of wood on the way back. In the open, with no barriers, I savored the breeze, turned my face to the sky, and inhaled the feeling of freedom. The same release I experienced when the opportunity arose to escape on my bike, or to the fields or woods.

I also experienced the same sense of liberation when my second-oldest sister and I helped manage the animal baits for my father's hunting resort. We drove the quad—loaded down with buckets of molasses, donuts, and bread—deep into the woods. Again I embraced the freedom that came with riding fast and the feeling of the wind on my flesh. Elation pounded in my chest. Reaching the sites, we went the rest of the way on foot. I didn't particularly like hiking into the baits because you never knew when a bear was lurking nearby. However, I relished the independence that came with these adventures. When we got the quad stuck, it gave us the chance to use our intellect to figure out how to get unstuck. When we took the wrong trail and got lost, we looked for landmarks to find our way. Again, I welcomed the experience of using my own brain and thrived in those moments. The invisible clutch of my parents and the oppression that came with it disappeared in nature.

In my teens, I recognized the depths of my father's demand for control. When we girls started to develop into women, we were no longer permitted to ride the quad because we had to straddle the machine to drive it, and the shape of our thighs might show and our breasts might bounce, drawing attention from men.

I later joked about the matter. I wasn't sure where all the predators they warned us about were because, when Dad's seasonal business was done for the year, there wasn't anyone around for miles. We lived so far back in the woods a car rarely drove by.

As my father's grip tightened, I yearned for the independence I had found in those moments in the woods. But internally, I belittled myself with a narrative that I was dirty and sinful for desiring to ride the quad when it would cause men to look at me with lust. So, in my mind, my body became my oppressor, like my parents and their God.

At the front of the church we attended at the time, a large pine sign read God is Love. I'd often look at the sign and try to remind myself that God was indeed that. Other times I would think that if the God they spoke of was love, I didn't need Him or this love. Their God was anything but love. He, like everything in life, was to be feared.

∞

I'm not sure when I understood that being financially secure provided freedom, but being an entrepreneur has always been in my blood; it's the place where I flourish.

Across from our house, growing up, there were fields with heaps of wild blueberries, and we older girls would pick the berries and attempt to sell them. On the odd occasion our extended family visited, we'd sell the berries to our aunts for two dollars a pint. I remember dreaming of all the money I could make and calculating the profit in my head. But, unfortunately, it never turned out as profitable as I hoped.

Around grade ten, for a short period, my father allowed me to tutor elementary kids after school. I loved it! I felt a sense of pride and purpose, and for the first time, I felt intelligent. I never felt smart.

The tutoring job was something of my very own, and I recall admiring *Revenue Canada* imprinted on the top of my first check. My chest expanded with satisfaction. I knew I was special then because the government was paying me. But before I'd received more than one or two paychecks, the job ended. I have no recollection why, but assume it was my parents' doing. During high school, I asked if I could get a job at a local convenience store as a cashier, but my father told me that I'd never work if I lived under his roof.

My father's desire for control extended to everyone in his life, not only his household. At times he was the most giving person ever, dropping off food to those in need and lending money he didn't have. Other times, I witnessed his manipulation. After I'd been married for almost a decade, my husband had become successful in business, but we needed a change, and for a brief time I considered moving closer to my family. My father jumped at the chance of having my husband work for him. We considered it for a minute, but as usual, it came with my dad's need to control. He informed us my husband would have to stay three provinces away, where the business was located, and our kids and I would have to remain near the family. Both my husband and I were not about to be manipulated. We declined his offer, prompting my father to quickly recant his words and say my children and I could go with my husband. But it was too late, because although time and distance had dulled my memory of how controlling he was, his behavior reminded me of what I would never again endure.

An incident between him and me in my graduating year spoke volumes about his need to master people. Graduation merchandise was being advertised at school, and I wanted to have the three-quarter length navy jacket more than anything I'd ever wanted as a youth. On the front it had the name of the high school, and on the opposite shoulder classmates were embroidering their names. I envisioned mine on the sleeve and can recall the urgency I felt to have my name for everyone to see. I wanted to be visible and to feel I mattered.

It was a safer bet to ask my mother for the jacket because she could do the dirty work and ask my father, because I never would. My plan backfired when she told me that if I wanted the coat, I would have to ask. And as scary as it was to approach him on any matter, or to be in the same room with him, I wanted the jacket. I had daydreamed of it for weeks. So, one morning before the bus came, I gathered the courage to approach him. He perched on a high counter stool, and my mother stood at his side. I swallowed back the nerves and asked. He gave me a cheeky grin, and a glint shone in his eyes as he relished my uneasiness. I figured he had been warned. I will never forget the punch in the gut I felt as the words fell from his lips: "If you want the coat, get on your knees and beg for it."

That day, pride and determination erupted in me, and I looked at him and said, "I don't need the coat." Then I whirled on my heel and walked out the front door and boarded the bus. Tears of frustration and disheartenment slipped down my cheeks, and I turned to stare out the window as the bus bounced along the old dirt road.

I did receive the jacket, and wore it until it was unfit to wear.

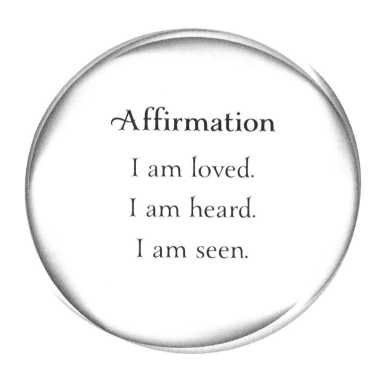

Affirmation

I am loved.

I am heard.

I am seen.

15–THE SIMMER

"Oppressed people cannot remain oppressed forever.
The yearning for freedom eventually manifests itself." ~
Martin Luther King Jr.

By the age of fifteen, I knew I had to get out of my parents' home. I didn't know how I could leave, but I knew if I didn't, I'd die a metaphysical death. I felt my spirit dying, replaced with simmering rage. But something inside me told me to get my education and graduate first. As the following years went by, my anger ticked like a faulty boiler. Although I lashed out at my siblings at times, for the most part, I kept my emotions in check and never swayed from my parents' teachings out of fear of punishment and damnation.

As my interest in boys developed, I noticed another shift and divide between my father's parenting of my two older sisters and me. They were allowed to speak to boys without his hawk-like gaze on them. Also, they were permitted freedoms and other luxuries I was not. The year before I graduated, I was surprised when my parents allowed Sara to attend her grand march, the first part of the prom before the dancing. She had a fancy dress made, walked with a boy, and had professional pictures done. I lived through her experience and daydreamed about my turn the following year. I had the color and design of the dress I would wear fashioned in my head, and knew the guy I would take. But when it came to my turn, my father said I couldn't attend.

For me, talking to guys in the churchyard or on the phone wasn't permitted. I spent a month of Sundays sitting in the van after church because I had stood, in broad daylight for all to see, speaking to a guy. There was no explanation for the so-called wrong I'd done, but being denied social connection hurt the worst. I recall the ache inside in the weeks to come as other young people gathered in circles, chatting and laughing as I sat holed up in the van.

Another time, years prior, when my parents turned the family room into a church and hosted a Sunday picnic after service, I was restricted to my room in the attic for a reason I don't recall. I remember feeling physically ill as, from the attic window, I observed the spread on the tables stretching across the lawn, and people mingling and laughing. Again, the segregation felt crippling. I had experienced what it felt like to be left out at school because I was different. I was accustomed to sitting in the library at lunch hour or walking the halls alone. But the degree of isolation, unworthiness, and embarrassment I felt when separated from people who looked like me had a more significant impact because my connection with other people was so limited.

The fire in my belly, and the need to be free of the pervasive fear, took hold in the last year of high school. I didn't know how much more I could take. Then, a few days before I graduated, I had a vivid dream that shook me to the very core. I dreamed I had harmed my parents. Although violence wasn't my way, the dream terrified me because I was aware of the simmering rage that had fueled it.

In hindsight, I believe the dream came to me as a warning

that I needed to leave; not because I would harm my parents, but because I needed to be free from their oppression.

As I walked the aisle to take my position on the stage on graduation night, I felt pride like I'd never experienced before. I had done it. While other classmates smiled and dreamed of a bright future and going off to college and university, my dream of furthering my education had been scared out of me. Instead, I had carried my own vision of my future, one I had held in my heart for years. Once I graduated, I would leave my parents' house and my hometown and never return. Three days later, I did precisely that, but I won't get ahead of myself. Let me tell you how I accomplished a task that required courage the like of which I had never displayed before.

To earn my freedom from the bondage of my parents, I would have to enter the lion's den and take on the beast himself.

It happened one Sunday after morning service, where again I was removed from social interaction by my dad, and again for talking to the young people, including a boy. He told me I had to sit in one of the Sunday school rooms until evening service, which would commence in four to five hours. Between services, people from out of town, like us, gathered in the main lobby to eat and for fellowship. I sat in the room, listening to their laugher and chatter, and the simmering anger inside me ignited. I paced the room as it built, and when a family friend who was my age popped her head in the door and asked why I wasn't hanging with the others, I quickly filled her in. She, like most, was aware of my father's ways, as her father had been on the receiving end of my father's need to control. Whatever she said that day caused the volcano inside me to erupt, and convinced by her words, I said, "You know what? I'm done." I marched from the room, and she hurried after me.

"Where are you going?" I heard panic in her voice.

"I don't know, but far away from him." Adrenaline fueled me as I stormed out the front doors of the tabernacle and made my way across the churchyard to the main road. She raced to keep up. Although we have lost contact over the years, I thank her for standing at my side and giving me the courage to defy my father. I kept walking down that road and couldn't have been gone five minutes before I looked over my shoulder and saw my parents' van coming up behind us.

I set my jaw in determination, and stifled the panic, and set my eyes on the horizon. I wasn't going back.

The van drove alongside us, and my dad rolled down the window, and said in a firm tone, "Get in the van."

I shook my head and turned to look straight ahead. "I'm not going home. I can't."

"Naomi, get in the van!" My mother's voice held a sudden authority she'd never mustered before.

I remember being agitated by the whine in her tone.

My ally, who had always been a firecracker, said with gusto, "She said she isn't going!"

But then my steps froze as my baby sister, eight at the time, opened the back window and pleaded with me. Fear and tears echoed in her voice. "Please, Naomi, don't leave."

And for a moment, I realized that I was leaving them behind, unprotected and alone.

I swallowed back the guilt and said, "I can't."

At that, my dad drove away, and my little sister's weeping drifted from the open windows.

For years I carried the guilt of leaving them behind. I didn't have a plan, just $150 to my name, which I'd received graduation gifts. I had no home and nowhere to go. I had thrown myself into a world I had no insight about, only fear.

I learned to suppress the guilt of abandoning my little sisters and of my parents' shame and disappointment in me. The ties to my family suffered greatly after that, and my accessibility to my siblings was limited. When my sisters would act up, my parents' hurt and disappointment echoed in their words: "You are just like Naomi." I could never grasp what was so horrible about me until I learned it wasn't me. My parents' love came with conditions.

In later years, my youngest sister came back to me and said, "It's thanks to you that he stopped beating us. After that day, he never touched us again."

Tears clotted in my throat at her words. Her confirmation that life had gotten better for them helped me shed the guilt of the hardest decision I had made in hopes of claiming my freedom. I forgave myself for abandoning them.

For the longest time, I contemplated if I had gone about leaving home the right way because of the distress to my little sisters and the hurt I caused my parents, but I came to terms with the fact. I had no other choice if I wanted to be free. I had to take my chances, and it came at a cost. As a result, I became a lone wolf and was estranged from my family.

16–THE OPPRESSOR

"As I'd seen over and again, people who see themselves as victims sometimes don't notice when they become oppressors."
~ **Souad Mekhennet**

"I imagine one of the reasons people cling to their hates so stubbornly is because they sense, once hate is gone, they will be forced to deal with pain." ~ **James Baldwin,** *The Fire Next Time*

After leaving home, I moved in with an African lady from my church for a few months before taking the nanny job on the army base. When I decided the job was no longer for me, I packed a suitcase with all I owned, which wasn't much, and boarded a flight west. I remember the day I stepped off the plane that October afternoon and the bite of the cold through my shoes. My husband, who was my boyfriend at the time, picked me up at the airport, and as we drove through the city I regarded the skyscrapers and tall glass buildings, and stifled the overwhelming desire to flee. Living on my parents' homestead, then moving to a smaller city, had been one thing, but the grander size of the new city left me feeling like a fish out of water.

For the next four to five years, I floundered in the religious dogma of my youth until I decided to live life the way that resonated with me. I could no longer follow a doctrine I didn't believe in and wouldn't do so to win my parents' approval, nor to avoid the criticism of family or the church. I spent years trying to sever the fear and brainwashing of what I would suffer if I didn't follow the "one way" teachings.

The desire to attend college took a back seat when I got pregnant with my son a few months into my marriage. A love like I never experienced before took hold, and I knew I wanted to give him my all. So I put all my effort into what success meant to me: a healthy marriage and being the best mother I could be.

When I suffered my first panic attack in my early twenties, the symptoms lasted a week straight. It was as though I couldn't snap out of the fight-or-flight response. During the first days, I had a metallic taste in my mouth, my vision was clouded, and it was as though all my senses had frozen—something had snapped in me, and I was terrified.

At the time, I ran a day home and had my own two small children. I immediately shut it down without considering the parents because I believed whatever had broken inside me needed fixing. Lacking adult support and desperate to regain control of my life, I asked my parents for help. My mom told me I had to get right with God, and it was His way (punishment and, again, fear-based living) of turning me back to Him, which, of course, only escalated my fear. Then she handed the phone over to my father because he was who the family turned to for guidance, and he also counseled people in his ministry. Desperate to be free of anxiety, I managed to set my fear for him aside in hopes of receiving help. I wouldn't say I harvested any guidance from the conversation, but he quoted a statement, "The greatest battle ever fought is in your mind," which stayed in my mind for years. The meaning in the quote for "believers" relates to the devil getting to you through your mind.

After speaking to my parents that day, I did what I had learned. I took my children's hands and led them to my room. We knelt beside my bed, and I prayed like I had never prayed before. Although I never understood the wrong in my transgressions, I begged God to help me get right and save me from myself and my wickedness. I asked Him to take away the desire to wear makeup and pants, cut my hair, and watch TV.

I rose from my bedside feeling empty but determined to fight to be "good" in the sense of my upbringing. An endeavor that didn't last because the tenets of my parents weren't authentic to me. I never turned my back on God, but I was determined not to be scared into serving an entity.

It is our birthright to think freely and connect to what feels authentic to us. What good does it do to blindly follow a belief system if you only do it for others? When voting, most know who they will vote for because the politicians' promises are something they believe in. With religion, I have witnessed repeatedly children who will continue in the faith of their parents because that is what they know. And some genuinely believe it and do it for themselves. But when it's for someone else, and not because it's your belief, you become a number of the faith and nothing more. Witnessing the scars of the youth who have left the religion I was raised in fills me with great sorrow. So many have blocked out all sense of self and spirituality because of the dismantling of their spirit through perpetual criticism, ingrained fear, and worthlessness.

My mistrust of men, instilled by my father and men's traditional role in the church, filled me with determination to never be controlled by men. The lack of control in my youth caused me to bristle at any situation where I thought I was restricted, and at times, I was a disservice to myself. I had to remove the trained fear that men were out to physically harm or dominate me. And, as mentioned, any communications with people of any faith put me on guard because of my experience with elders and members of the churches I attended, where they were judgmental and often hypocritical. With the desire to not turn God out of my life, but being leery of any fanaticism, I tried out other faiths, which was a better experience. However, in the end, I decided organized religion wasn't for me and adapted my own belief system that resonates with me.

This is where it gets complicated. Humans often create a divide if we don't see eye to eye on politics, religion, and other topics. We have conditioned ourselves to become offended if someone sees life differently from us. As an observer, and someone who doesn't like conflict, I used to brace when people would bring up politics and religion because, in my experience, these matters led to belittlement, raised voices, and frustration between the parties. However, we demonstrate kindness and compassion to the highest degree when we can drop the "savior" or "judgmental" mentality and allow others to grasp what resonates with them without the need to be correct. After all, what is it to us if someone sees life differently? Who nominated us as judge and jury?

One of my dad's notorious sayings was "Even when I'm wrong, I'm right." The need to be right is the self-centered whining of the ego, revealing its fear of what will happen to itself if declared wrong.

The absence of authority over my own life growing up caused me to be mindful of the plights of others. As a result,

I've learned respect for all because I experienced how it feels to not be respected, seen, or heard.

As a child, when my parents stood over me, informing me of all that was wrong with me, I recall my psyche crying out, "I'm not those things. I'm not. I'm good."

During my journey to discovering myself and freeing the little girl buried under the rubble life became too hard at times, and the desire to flee or shut down arose. I often said to my husband, "I don't want to shut down because if I do, I fear I will lose myself entirely." The worry of losing myself or becoming isolated guided my life.

The longer I suppressed my personal truth and downplayed what happened in my childhood at the hands of family members, anger continued to simmer in my subconscious. On rare occasions, I erupted with anger that would come out of nowhere. I managed to keep a lid on my emotions in the presence of outsiders, but when my children or husband pushed my triggers, I would go from 0 to 100. Then, instantly, I would be filled with regret. I was aware of my behavior and, guided by how my parents never apologized or held themselves accountable, I would sit my children down, tell them I was sorry, and explain that my outburst had nothing to do with them. "It was me," I'd say. "I messed up. Parents are human, too. Because we are parents doesn't mean we know everything. I'm simply doing the best I know how."

These outbursts would stay with me, and I would condemn myself for my lack of control over my emotions. But I had no clue how to uproot the anger and pain buried deep inside me. After all the work I had done in talk therapy, why did my past still have hold of me? I was sick of talking about it; I just wanted to be free.

Self-Sabotage

An old massage therapist I connected with because we talked about life on a more profound level once shared how, in her late teens or early twenties, someone had said to her, "You aren't that special that everything someone thinks or does is about you." I remember being taken aback by a statement I considered harsh for an older person to say to a younger, more impressionable, person. However, she went on to say how she had absorbed the comment and applied it positively to her life.

It wasn't about the adult saying she wasn't special, because she was, but about giving your power away. When we get caught up in our emotions and past experiences that impact us negatively, we become our own oppressors. Everything that happens around us and to us doesn't mean that it is about us. When trolls and haters fire at you with all their hate and venom, who is it really about? Should their opinions hold any value? No, so we need not absorb it because it has nothing to do with you. Their hate is their wounds requiring healing. When I understood this, the haters who came after me no longer had a hold over me. The deep piercing I once felt, which would dampen my spirit and leave me spinning, became a prick, which quickly dissipated.

We can't avoid criticism or hate. But differentiating between healthy criticism and toxicity is the key.

Food for Thought

Often we react with anger, or project feelings of inadequacy on others, feeling oppressed by our communities when, in fact, we have become our own oppressors. But we carry a belief that it's they who are to blame for the oppression we feel. Eleanor Roosevelt is believed to have once said,

"No one can make you feel inferior without your consent." The quote holds merit.

So often, we become our own oppressors because we conform to the biases of others, or our own jaded perceptions constructed from past experiences that dictate and often hinder all new ones. We become our own stumbling blocks. Sometimes we just need to get out of our own way and get to the root of the issue. Why are we allowing others to make us feel inferior?

Sara, the sister born fifteen months before me, was book smart, and I considered her a genius. Often, in my school years, I walked in her shadow. Teachers lacking perception of the impact their words made on me would say, "Wow, you sure wouldn't know you were Sara's sister." I heard these statements on several occasions from two male teachers who admired her brilliance. Where I escaped into my imagination and writing fiction, she buried herself in books, looking to seek my parents' approval and that of her teachers. She would cry if she didn't receive 100% on her test, while I patted myself on the back for my 70–80% average. On her graduation night, I remember sitting in the audience, and hearing the speaker say, "And the award goes to Sara" or "And the scholarship goes to Sara." I remember thinking how unfair it was to the other students and wondering if she would gobble up all the rewards.

From the comments of these teachers, and for the reasons I shared in chapter two, I came to believe that I wasn't smart. The taunting from my dad about my curves and the ridicule about my body caused me to use human shields in all photos with me in them. I would hide at the back, or if seated on a couch for a photo, I'd grab a pillow to hide my extra fluff.

The depth of my personal growth became apparent in a branding photoshoot I had done. Usually I would put a ton of pressure on myself, worrying about how they would turn out.

Would I look fat? What if I didn't like them? I would spend lots of time sorting through outfits and matching accessories to control the outcome the best I could. This time, I put my time into staging my home where the pictures were to be taken. As I went about placing items that added a pop of color, re-flected my brand, or were what I wanted to show the world, I silently soothed the need to control how the photos turned out. If I got one picture that turned out, I'd be happy. So what if the public saw I wasn't at my ideal weight. I'm working on myself and standing in my truth. I would not hide.

During the shoot, the photographer offered instructions that I should act playful and carefree, and at one point sug-gested I place a pillow in front of myself. Inside, I braced. Although I followed her instructions, I have yet to use the picture with the pillow. She didn't suggest it because she thought I needed to cover up, but her direction made me aware of the girl I no longer was.

Affirmation

I am stepping out of
my own way. I am dealing
with the pain of what keeps
me the oppressor
in my life.

17–THE CAGE SPRUNG OPEN

"Perfectionist parents seem to operate under the illusion that if they can just get their children to be perfect, they will be a perfect family. They put the burden of stability on the child to avoid facing the fact that they, as parents, cannot provide it. The child fails and becomes the scapegoat for family problems. Once again, the child is saddled with the blame." ~ **Susan Forward, PhD,** *Toxic Parents: Overcoming Their Hurtful Legacy and Reclaiming Your Life*

The call arrived in the middle of the night.

"Naomi…" The hollowness and anxiety in my oldest sister's voice echoed over the phone.

"Yeah. What is it?" I blinked into the darkness, noting the time on the alarm clock.

"It's Dad. H-he's gone."

"Gone?" I sat up in bed, my brain still in a sleep-induced fog. My mind scrambled to make meaning of what she was saying. My grandparents recently moved closer to my parents, and I thought she referred to my grandfather.

"Yeah." Her tone was robotic. "He preached a good sermon today…"

I jumped out of bed, becoming aware that someone

significant had died. She continued to speak, but I retained nothing because my mind was on my grandfather. She had to be talking about him. He had battled with stomach cancer, but the doctors had removed it. He didn't preach, so who was she referring to?

"Wait a minute. Who died?" My heart raced as I paced the floor, awaiting an answer.

"Dad."

"My dad?" I froze, and my stomach dropped.

My husband sat up. "Babe, what is it?"

"My dad…I think…" I stared into the dark, numbness washing over me.

My dad died on a Sunday from a blood clot that traveled from his groin to his heart. He had been deemed the pillar of strength in the family, and his death turned our world upside down.

Some months before my father's sudden death, he had gone to the doctor a couple of times because he hadn't been feeling well. He proudly told us all that the doctor said he was a "fine specimen of a man."

My baby sister was visiting me at the time and was set to return home the following day. The Friday evening before his death, she and I had sat on the couch talking. My phone rang, and I looked at it and noticed it was my dad. I chose to ignore the call, so he texted, referencing the phone call and saying in jest that I was ignoring him. That choice would become one of my greatest regrets. In the following years, I wondered, what if he had known something wasn't right? What if he sensed he might die? A few days before his death, my sister had mentioned that she had visited my parents before coming to see me and said his coloring had been off; I had dismissed it with a frown. What if he had been calling to fix what had never been repaired between us? And because of the choice to ignore his call, I would never have what I'd longed to hear all my life: I'm sorry. I didn't do right by you. It wasn't you. It was me.

The day I arrived at my parents' home to help with funeral arrangements, I wore pants into their house for the first time. Before my dad's passing, I tried to visit every two or three years and kept long skirts and long-sleeved tops tucked away in the closet for my trips to see family members. I told myself I had done it out of respect, but in truth, it was partially out of respect and fear of being shunned.

My relationship with my father had improved throughout my adult life. The first time I recall my father taking a stand for me was when it came to my marriage. I made the poor decision to have my wedding in the area where I grew up to be convenient for my husband's and my families. The pastor we originally asked to perform the ceremony was our old pastor. My family had moved away for a time, but had recently moved back to their hometown. The protocol at that particular church for anyone who had left was to consider them an outsider to be harshly ridiculed, even if they shared the same faith. After agreeing to marry us, the pastor returned with the request that I have a doctor's note proving I was a virgin, and if confirmed I wasn't, I would be required to wear colors to display to my wedding guests my assumed disgrace. I brought the matter to my father, and he told me whether I was or wasn't was nobody's business and arranged to have a different pastor marry me, closer to my hometown.

The man who married us took my husband and I into his office, and I will never forget the words he told my husband. He said, "If I can tell you one piece of marriage advice, it is this: remember, she is your queen, and the home is her palace." The gentle way he encouraged us to succeed, when many never believed my husband and I would make it, remained with me. As did my father's willingness to stand up for me at a time that should've been happy but had been overtaken with drama and too many people's opinions and emotions.

Some years into my marriage, my father had gone away on business, and upon his return, he called me and told me he had stumbled across a poem he wanted to read to me. I don't know how the verse went, but somewhere in it was the word "sorry." I understood at that time that although his pride wouldn't allow him to admit his wrongs, it was his way of apologizing, and for the time, it was enough for me to accept his olive branch—a hairline fracture formed in the fortress I had built to keep him at bay.

However, when grandchildren came on the scene, I witnessed a vastly different man than the one who had fathered me.

Once, he'd flown in to visit my sister and I and to see his only two grandsons at the time. In those years, I practiced the time-out method in parenting and placed my two-year-old son in his oversized orange-fur tiger chair. He sat howling, with big crocodile tears, and kicking up a fuss. My dad opened his arms wide and said, with the biggest grin on his face, "Come to Papa."

My son bolted across the living room and jumped into his arms while I stood back, gobsmacked. Who was this man and what had he done with my father?

During that visit, he arranged for us all to go on several fun outings with the kids. It was as though he wanted to savor every moment. I agreed to the zoo because that was all I could afford at the time. I brought a baggie of coins and stood at the admissions window, painstakingly counting out each one. I was embarrassed that he and my other family stood watching, but I didn't want to say no to going, and I wasn't about to tell them I couldn't afford to go. I didn't even have a five-dollar bill to my name because I was a stay-at-home mom, and my husband barely made $10 an hour. I'm sure my family figured it out, but in my mind, my pride remained intact. No one would know our struggles as young married parents to make ends meet.

Another time, when I visited my parents, they didn't have much in their cupboards or easily accessible food to give my children, so I went to town and purchased groceries. My father took me aside and said that I was never to buy food when I came to his house. I can only assume it was a matter of pride because it was a trait that often overshadowed his judgment.

To say he was a better grandfather than a father is an understatement. It was like his grandkids could do no wrong. I recall visiting them and coming back to their acreage from shopping in town with my sister. Dad stood outside by the front door with two of his grandsons, one being my six-year-old. He called me over, and I noted the broad grin on his face. He proceeded to reveal how my son had taught his younger grandson to smoke with sticks. I wanted the ground to swallow me up, and I feared my son would receive my father's disapproval. I didn't want my kids to ever feel rejected, as I had felt with my parents. My son hadn't been around smokers, but he had learned it somewhere, as I had when I was younger. Dad pointed at the twig in my son's hand and said, "Show your mom how you taught Sam to smoke." The stoic man who would've whipped my backside as a kid for pretending to smoke was beside himself with amusement.

The few times we visited, my dad went all out arranging all sorts of fun actives for the kids and taking them to the store to purchase toys. In addition, he treated me with generosity, kindness, and more love than I had ever received growing up. It was as though he endeavored to make up for past behaviors.

Still, whenever I called my parents' house, I quickly asked for my mother. I sensed it hurt him, but I didn't know how to communicate because my fear of him was rooted so deep. Although I'd decided he would no longer be the puppet master of my life, I fooled myself into thinking he no longer had a hold on me. However, I never let him close to me. I avoided being left alone in the same room or car with him. I smiled and extended kindness and respect while never revealing the anxiety churning my gut. I physically felt my hackles rise in his presence, as I expected the father of my youth to emerge.

Married with two kids, I was again visiting my family, and my father sent one of my sisters to fetch me. My heart sped up when I heard the dreaded, "Naomi, Dad wants you." An invisible hand seized my throat as I immediately began racking my brain for what I could have done or said wrong. I worried all the way to the basement, and when I found him he smiled and told me something lighthearted.

Five years before Dad's death my husband and I had started our first business, and we were doing well. We were about to take our kids to Mexico when Dad called and said he wanted to speak to my husband and me. The fear I associated with him reared its head. What could he possibly want to talk to me about? Had I done something I wasn't aware of? I raced through memories of the past few days, and the week, and came up empty-handed. When he wanted to add my mother to the conversation, my mind ran to the only possible conclusion. They were getting a divorce. Although divorce was forbidden, it could be the only possible reason for the serious undertone. Then, when he asked to borrow money, you could have blown me over. My throat seized up, and numbness took hold. What? How could he need money? His advice on how my husband and I should run our business was free-flowing—although I had never heeded his advice because I had put up a block between him and me.

I wasn't open to any advice he offered but considered him to be an innovative businessman. It was at this moment I sensed a vulnerability in him. Pride was my father's demon. If he had humbled himself enough to ask me, of all people, for money, I knew he was desperate. Anxiety rose. If he didn't have money, what would I do? After leaving home, I had never asked him for anything but figured that if something happened to my husband and I needed help, I'd turn to him. The thought had comforted me. I would've had to be down and out to ask for money, especially from him. I had decided by this point I would never rely on anyone in life but my husband. My husband had set out alone in life at sixteen, and me at eighteen. We had created a life of our choosing, and I considered us a power team. We had taken on the world alone, and I thought I liked it that way. Like my father, I had a lot of pride.

My father had been a hard worker all his life. Unfortunately, due to the recession in the US, his business had started to fail. He was swimming in debt but never let on. The fact that he was struggling caused me uncertainty. If the man I had imagined as powerful could break, what did it mean for me? One of my biggest fears in those years was proving I was what I believed they thought I was: a failure. I would not fail! And, like my dad, no one was going to know if I was struggling.

I agreed to help him but suggested we ask my other married sisters to help because it was a significant amount. His pride bruised, he instantly became enraged and told me to forget it. He didn't need my help. Of course, I felt guilty and obligated, but I wasn't willing to hand over all the money I had managed to save, so behind his back, I enlisted two other sisters to help me give him the money he needed. I suggested that, to protect his pride and my backside, we keep it just between us.

I sent him the money, and he told me he would pay me back. But, unfortunately, he never paid the money back because his business never recovered, and time wasn't in his favor.

A year or two before his passing he called me, and I recall standing in the kitchen. He said, "I'm proud of the person you've become. You've done well for yourself. You've done a good job at raising your children." His words melted my heart a little more.

The afternoon I stood over my father's casket with my sisters and Mom, and they stood in their grief, I swallowed back the guilt. Eyes dry, I regarded the form lying before me, appearing like a wax replica of my father. I should be crying. I should feel something, I told myself. But numbness gripped me. My sisters' murmurs of sorrow and farewells whispered around me. *For god's sake, Naomi, this is your father. Say something,* I ridiculed myself. So my lips parted, and my farewell to the man who had been the boogeyman came out. "I'm sorry I couldn't be what you wanted me to be."

For years, I judged myself for the words I said, believing they were disingenuous and shallow. However, they were all I had to give. I reflected on the divide that had defined our relationship. I considered the wasted time and how we both would've thrived if we had repaired the damage. Unfortunately, he never seemed to have the tools, and I never gathered them in my trips to therapy or personal growth. I desired a relationship that simply would never be, and I grieved for that.

As shocking as it sounds, over the next couple of years, I realized my father's death sprung open the cage around my soul, and I took flight. The liberation I felt left me with a ton of guilt.

After his death, my battles with my mother began. I became

angry at my father for leaving us with a woman who had no life experience, and at times I considered her downright entitled and selfish. His financial ruin and lack of life insurance had left my mother with nothing.

Why was it I who had been left to clean up his mess? The one daughter he had treated with such contempt as a child. The child he had never deemed worthy until she had financially made something of herself. I was enraged! It wasn't fair. Consumed with the pressure of my mother's situation and wallowing in self-pity, anger, and feeling overwhelmed, I again sought therapy.

This time, I got advice that would start the journey to healing concerning my father. The therapist told me to write a letter to my father. She told me to write one saying what I would say to him if he were still alive, and another stating what I believed he would say back. I recall thinking it wouldn't work. Again, how could something so simple heal all my pain? No therapy had helped before, but I was game to try anything because I desperately wanted to be whole.

The day I decided I would take her advice, I made a coffee and sat outside. That sunny summer afternoon, the tears flowed and melded with the words that poured onto the pages. I released the pain and longing for a father I had always wanted. I dismantled the fortress around my heart because he was gone and no longer a threat. I let go of years of resentment and desire to be heard, seen, and loved by him. Our time to mend our relationship could never be, but that day I gave my father grace and let his hold on me go.

I still bore many childhood wounds. Someone suggested reading the book *You Can Heal Your Life* by Louise Hay. The parts of the book where she speaks about self-love and the inner child hit me hard. Through her work, I gathered the critical tools

I've been searching for all my life. I learned about affirmations, what self-love really was, and how to apply it to my life. She also suggested seeing your parents as children and what they may have faced in their young lives. More healing needed to occur with the trauma left behind by my father, so I imagined him as a little boy. What had he gone through in his life to become a man who didn't trust, felt he needed to control every aspect of his life, and caused him to administer his children with cruelty and abuse?

The concept of the inner child led me to heal my own while looking at my parents as children. What were their stories? In my evaluation, I had to revisit my childhood first.

I never formed a bond with my parents, and if, perhaps, in the first years of life I had, somewhere along the way the bond was broken. However, I remember occasions when it wasn't so bad, times before fear took root. When I was the baby of the family, he would play hide and go seek with my two older siblings and me. He'd place me on a shelf and tell me to stay quiet. I recall photos of me around this time, dressed up with a feather headdress and a holster around my waist, and how my eyes gleamed like those of a happy child. When I was around eight or ten, he took me on the back of his Ski-Doo to check his traps. He took me bass fishing and stopped at the convenience store by the river to buy a snack consisting of bananas and a block of cheese, which was a luxury in our house. It felt special, and I don't recall a sense of fear.

During one of these fishing trips, my dad paddled our canoe to shore and told me to get out. So I did precisely that. I leaped onto the dock and heard a yelp from my dad and the swoosh of the water. I looked back as he surfaced and stood waist-deep in the water. His eyes flashed with annoyance. I thought I had done it for sure then, but he simply gathered his gear, turned the canoe upright, and pulled it from the water. I lived to face another day.

As a kid, I helped him with the piping under the house. I scurried on my belly behind him to pass the tools. In these moments, he often seemed on edge and would be snappy when I didn't hand him the right tool. Another time he asked me to help him carry a washer from the old house to the new place, which was about a hundred yards away. I wanted to please him. I was determined not to let him down but I struggled with the machine, until I couldn't hold up my end any longer. I again earned his frustration, which came in words of annoyance and the flash of his green eyes. As a kid, I didn't understand that the frustrations I often witnessed in him had nothing to do with me and everything to do with him.

Like me, I believe my father isolated himself in life and tried to control his surroundings. Although we went about it in entirely different ways, I realized the commonality we shared.

These not-so-bad times caused me to inquire how he was capable of being the not-so-good guy. Dad never talked about his upbringing. I would consider his family prideful and hushed when it came to family affairs. My paternal grandmother came from lovely parents, I'm told. Late in my life, I found out my grandmother had been married before she married my grandfather. During her first marriage, her husband openly cheated on her, which was well-known around town. She carried the pain into her marriage with my grandfather, in which she would suffer the same treatment. In the early years of her marriage to him, he was a heavy drinker. I can only imagine the hurt she experienced. I briefly remember my grandfather during these years but recall the quieter, more reserved man he became.

In my father's death, his truth is silenced. And with both

of my paternal grandparents gone, I can only rely on family stories. There are accounts of the cruelty between my grandfather and his horde of brothers, as there are several stories of cruelty between my father and his siblings. One can assume he transferred his inflicted wounds to us girls.

I recall my father saying to me once, "You have to wear sunglasses, or you will get wrinkles." I remember frowning at him and thinking it was a bizarre thing for a man to say, and perhaps something my mother would say, as women tend to dread the wrinkles that come with age. But while writing this book the thought returned to me, like it has several times over the years. At times, I wondered if beauty was essential to my father and enforced his need for perfection in his daughters. He was handsome and charismatic. I recall him coming to school once and how a female teacher blushed and fluffed her hair on his arrival. Another time, a female classmate dashed into the classroom after lunch, all excited and flushed. "I just saw your dad driving through town," she said before flopping down into her chair with a dreamy look on her face. Other classmates would note how good-looking my father was, and of course, I thought they were ridiculous. He was my father. And fathers aren't handsome. Then I grew up and realized my father was indeed an attractive man.

I've heard stories about how his mother, my grandmother, was considered one of the most beautiful women in the county. But, with the infidelity of her husbands, had she struggled with insecurities and feelings of not being perfect enough, and somehow my father acquired a belief that you had to be attractive or you were devalued somehow? Or was it when one of my father's younger sisters got hit by a truck and had to undergo several surgeries to repair her face, and he witnessed the attention that went into that sister to ensure her face was perfect. Because I recall that when my baby sister did a face-plant in the churchyard in Tennessee, my dad was more disconcerted than my mother. When my daughter was fifteen months old, she also did a face-plant before we went to visit my parents, and my father was visibly upset and told me I had to be more careful that she didn't damage her face.

On further consideration, my father and his sister, who had gotten injured, had a toxic relationship until he died. I wonder, did it develop because he became jealous over the attention she received from my grandparents as they focused on her recovery? My sisters and I are aware that my mother favors our sister, who has had multiple back surgeries since the age of age twelve. My son mentioned how everything in our house was about our daughter because of her dramatics and being bullied. I believe, when a parent's attention turns more to one child over another because of situations outside of a parent's control, sibling rivalry for parents' attention can ensue.

Forgiveness

Despite my father's faults, I saw his growth and a tenderness I'd never witnessed while growing up in the last years of his life. My empathy and observations made me want to forgive him. I loved my dad. And, as sad as it is, I feel closer to him in his death.

One day last year, I stood alone in my kitchen preparing the evening meal and reflecting on my dad and our relationship. A feeling overcame me to speak to my dad. I paused my knife on the cutting board and said, "I'm sorry for the pain I caused you. Please forgive me...and, I forgive you."

The final piece of healing concerning my dad felt

complete. I forgave myself for any self-imposed guilt and him for any unknown residue that remained.

In reflection, I draw comfort that my dad chose to take me to his favorite places on the water and in nature. It was there he relaxed and appeared at peace, and it was there I harvested positive memories with him.

I believe he didn't know what to do with me when my body changed from a child to a woman.

I've come to understand he loved me the best he knew how. But I acknowledge that he required the tools to heal himself and perhaps, like me, he had felt alone and vulnerable.

18–THE LONE WOLF

"The hardest walk you can make, is the walk you make alone, but that is the walk that makes you the strongest." ~ **Fearless Motivation**

The lone wolf wandered into my life in my thirties and changed it forever. James, known as Jimmy and affectionately referred to by my husband, my children, and me as Jimmy Boy, was an ex-airborne military man. He had an infectious laugh that reverberated throughout a room and instantly brought a smile to your lips. I observed the rigid set of his jaw and the stiffness of his pose, but perceived the underlying kindness at his core.

My husband and he initially developed a relationship. They had met through work and quickly came to respect each other. Eventually, my husband considered them friends enough that, when he was in the area, he stopped by Jimmy's home with coffee. However, that didn't go over so well. A relationship at work had been safe enough, but allowing my husband into his personal life was another matter. In time, however, my husband earned his trust and their relationship flourished. Then, as Jimmy's walls came down, he met our children and me.

Over time, he started showing up at our house bright and

early on Sunday mornings with coffee and muffins or donuts. He sought to please us at every turn, and we him. My kids loved him, and although he wasn't blood he became a father figure to my husband and I and a grandfather to my children. He went to their activities and held a genuine interest in what happened in their lives. He was everything family is supposed to be, and to us, the sun rose and set on him.

As time passed and our bond strengthened, we learned of the little boy who still guarded his heart against the reprimands of his deceased father, the stoic man he called "the sergeant." As he shared stories, I developed a strong connection with him. He was born into a family of boys, and he was the youngest. He considered the brother ahead of him intelligent, unlike himself. His mother was firm but gentle, and he had a relationship with her until she died. In his childhood, his father traveled a lot for business. His paternal grandfather was part of the Senate, and the environment of his family home was martial. Jimmy struggled to fit in, and dropped out of high school without telling his parents and got a job. When his father found out, he shipped him off to military school.

Jimmy called himself a rebel, continually creating chaos. For a reason I can't recall, he was thrown into military prison, and one of his superiors visited him and told him he was either going to rot in there or enroll in the Canadian Airborne Regiment. And it was there that he would find his chosen family. He quickly moved up the ladder and excelled. He traveled to different countries and experienced life through another lens. He embraced cultures and people's ways of living with keen respect and admiration, which I connected to because of my beliefs that we are all equal and bring beauty to the world. He was the most nonjudgmental person I knew, and I loved that about him.

He allowed everyone to be themselves without putting them in boxes of what he considered suitable.

He married a military lady, and soon after he retired from the army, he started his own business. He spoke of his love for his wife and for the daughter they shared. However, with his mindset to prove himself to the world, he put his all into his business and worked long hours. He admitted he had a temper, and work came before his family. When their daughter was one, he and his wife divorced. She moved two thousand miles away and took their daughter with her. The distance and the toxicity between him and his ex-wife caused him to become a stranger to his daughter. After trying to visit her a few times, and facing the child's rejection, he decided to guard his heart and removed himself from her life. A choice he came to regret, as over time he lost track of her. Later he tried to find them, to no avail.

As I listened to his story and observed him throughout the years, I realized he had placed himself in a self-imposed prison to avoid rejection, vulnerability, and hurt. Yet he acknowledged that some of the hardships he faced came at his own hand.

He had a brother that lived minutes away, but he felt he had done him dirty on one or more occasions and alienated him from his life. The other brother lived a few provinces away, and they had been what he considered close, yet they only saw each other two or three times in the forty-some years after leaving their parents' home. So the brotherhood he had formed with the airborne regiment became the family he connected with, and would remain so throughout his life.

He often visited his local mom-and-pop restaurant to visit with his friends and, later, he took us. When he walked in the door, the waitresses brightened and called out a greeting. He was the type who waltzed into a room with poise and friendliness, and no one was the wiser how guarded a man he indeed was.

As for the family I had created with my husband, Jimmy gave us his all. His attention and love came without conditions. He was our number-one fan. The fact that he could never pronounce my name correctly and called me "Yomi" endeared him even more to me. His compliments came effortlessly. He made statements like, "You're a good mother, Yomi." Or when I would send him home with care packages of food, he'd say, "You're one hell of a cook." The next time I would see him, he'd crow, "It was bloody awesome. Just bloody awesome." His praise and the value he held for me profoundly impacted my life. I looked up to him, and although I wasn't accustomed to asking for advice from others, on the odd occasion, I did ask him.

In 2012, he was diagnosed with pancreatic cancer, for which he had radiation. A year later, it came back in his colon, and he underwent surgery and was equipped with a colostomy bag. Stubbornness was one of his downfalls, and he went alone to the surgery and got a taxi home. He displayed the same character throughout his battle with cancer. He didn't want to have to depend on, or inconvenience, anyone. He was so set in his ways, he got the company who delivered his colostomy bags to throw them over the fence. He refused to have strangers or anyone who hadn't gained his trust into his house. He reminded me of Mr. Wilson on *Dennis the Menace* because some days he was plain old ornery.

Later, his cancer returned to his lungs, and he again underwent surgery. He started chemo and radiation, and we held the hope his cancer would go into remission. The nurses thought he was a hoot because he teased and joked with them throughout his chemo treatments. He'd say, with a chuckle, "Well, I have to go flirt with the ladies today" before informing us what a "bloody good job" the nurses did and that they provided him with the best of care. During his four years of fighting cancer, he never contacted his brothers to let them know. He also never let on to the few friends in his life until he couldn't hide it anymore. We were the only ones he allowed close enough to witness his struggle and vulnerability.

Dealing with a lot of stress of our own, my husband and I had planned a quick trip to California to get away. Toward the end of our four-day stay we received a panicked call from him, letting us know he was in the hospital. He hated hospitals and not being in control. He wanted us to come to the hospital, and wanted to know where we were and how long before we could get there. We hadn't told him we were going out of town but quickly informed him of our whereabouts and told him we'd book the next flight home.

We arrived at the hospital around 11:00 p.m. that evening, well past visiting hours, and inquired as to his whereabouts at the nursing station. The nurse brightened and said, "Yes, he has been anticipating your arrival all day. He talked nonstop about you."

We visited his room and found him lying against the pillows, looking weaker than usual. He stirred when we walked in and smiled when he recognized us. We spoke for a while, and I assured him I'd return the next day, as my husband couldn't get away from work. He nodded, and I observed the urgency in his eyes that I do exactly that. He handed me a card he had on his nightstand, which he had brought in his overnight bag.

Later we learned he had been in the shower when the onset of symptoms occurred, which frightened him enough to call an ambulance. And, Jimmy being Jimmy, he would've had to be in dire straits to request an ambulance. But before he called for help, he shaved, packed a bag, and sat down to write us the card. In true Jimmy style, the card stated how much he cared for us and appeared to be his goodbye; he later told us he thought this was his last dance. There was also a certified check for a substantial amount of money. I can only surmise that, as he sensed his time drawing closer, he had previously gone to the bank to get the draft, and purchased the card. At first we refused to take the money, but he insisted and refused to take it back. I didn't want him to think that he had to buy our time, love, or help.

The following day I returned to the hospital. The doctor suggested that, because he lived alone, he should go to assisted living, where he would have care. Panicked, he looked from the doctor to me with desperation in his eyes. "Yomi, what do you think we should do?"

My husband and I were up to our ears in stress and responsibility at this point in our lives. Not only did we have a family to raise, but we also had our businesses, the responsibility of my mom, and we were involved in an ongoing three-year court battle with our ex-business partner. I was at my breaking point but I knew Jimmy had no one, and he needed us.

I looked from him to the doctor and said, "He needs to be at home. That's where he will be the happiest. My husband and I will do whatever it takes to ensure he is taken care of. If one of us needs to move in with him, that is what we're willing to do."

The doctor agreed to the terms and released him into my care. And again, Jimmy being Jimmy, he allowed me to take him home but refused to let my husband or me move in with him. He didn't want to be a burden. So our trips to his home, which was forty minutes away, became more frequent. The following week we took him to a hospital three hours away for treatment on his brain. Here we learned that, even with the treatment, he would have another nine months at best.

After the treatment, we returned home. And soon after, he decided to stop chemo and radiation because he believed it robbed him of the quality he wanted in his last days.

Some weeks later, I went to the hospital with chest pain. A spot showed up on my lung, which prompted the doctor to request more intense testing. When they mentioned the possibility that the spot could be cancer, my world stopped. *But I'm not a smoker and never have been*, I thought. *So how could they even suggest lung cancer?* My anxiety went through the roof. I already dreaded going with Jimmy to his doctor appointments. My heart couldn't handle all the suffering. While we waited for him to be seen, I considered what the patients must be feeling. Were they scared? Did they have someone to care for them?

For a week straight, I suffered from panic attacks. I paced the floors and cried to my husband. He tried his best to comfort me and told me that, if I did have cancer, we would face it together. He had always been my rock, and although he tried to be strong for me I saw the worry in his eyes. I feared death more than anything, and the "C" word ranked high in my fears. Angry and distressed, I questioned God. *Why now? I am barely keeping my head above water, and now my health has been added to the list.*

Over the following weeks I visited several specialists, including a pulmonologist. I grappled with guilt because, during this time, the last thing I wanted to do was be around Jimmy or take him to doctor appointments. I wanted to be as far away from cancer as possible. At one point, I told my husband I needed him to care for Jimmy. That I couldn't do it. I struggled to simply show up in life each day, which caused massive guilt. I loved Jimmy, and he needed me. *How can you be so selfish?* I punished myself for what I classified as weakness. I wallowed for a spell until one day I decided: enough. If it was my turn to leave this world, I would make my days count. I wouldn't remain a prisoner of fear and anxiety. The attacks disappeared as I gathered strength from the greatest example I had in my life.

Jimmy walked through cancer with a heroic demeanor, never complaining, and making each day matter. He sprinkled laughter and merriment at his local diner, the grocery store, and with every interaction.

Thankfully, the tests came back and confirmed that I didn't have cancer.

In the last months of Jimmy's life, he decided that if he was going out, he'd do it with a red carpet rolled out. We moved heaven and earth to ensure he did precisely that.

It was during the last months that he often talked of his daughter and his regrets. He spoke of his desire to find her. But between suppressing his memories to cope with the heartache and the medicines he was on, he had difficulty remembering details about his ex-wife's family and where we could start looking. I noted the bits of information he gave me and asked if he wanted me to do some searching to see if I could locate them. He said we would. Tracking down people wasn't my forte, but my plan was to check the internet and get a copy of his marriage certificate because he couldn't recall his wife's maiden name.

At the registries, they required his signature to file the paperwork and told me it could be weeks before he received it in the mail. I quietly let them know he may not have weeks, but we filed it anyway. Over the following weeks, while we waited, he and I often talked about what he could remember, and I recorded every detail in my mind. At home, I'd search the internet for hours, usually into the early hours of the morning. Finally, coming up empty-handed, I contacted a private investigator, and he said with the few details I had to go on, we would be hunting for a needle in a haystack. But I couldn't accept there was no hope. I had to give Jimmy what he wanted more than anything, and that was his daughter. He didn't want to contact her because he didn't believe it was right to enter her life when he was about to make his exit. He only wanted to see her face and know what had become of her.

After much searching and disappointment, I felt hopeless. Then one day while I was visiting him, he gave me a name he had forgotten—the name of his ex-wife's brother. At home, I went on the hunt again. I managed to locate the brother in time, which led me to Jimmy's ex-wife and his daughter. She was a woman in her thirties, and the resemblance to her father was undeniable. My heart soared, and I leaned back in my chair and wept. I had found her.

The following day I arrived at his house bright and early and burst through the front door.

"I found her, Jimmy. I found your daughter."

His mouth dropped open, and his eyes gleamed with hope. "Are you sure?"

"Very sure," I said, digging through my purse for my phone. I pulled up her picture. "She is the spitting image of you!" I felt like my heart would burst as I handed him the phone.

He looked at the stranger in the image and didn't connect at first. I could tell he wasn't sure, and then when I showed him a picture of his ex-wife and his daughter, he immediately recognized her.

He smiled as he looked at his daughter. "Well, I'll be," he said with pride.

Often over the following days, when I showed up, he'd say,

"Yomi, can you show me her picture again?" And so I did. I sat and watched as yearning and regret played over his face.

While I was at work one day, he called me and told me to make sure I was sitting down. Then he started to cry (something I'd never seen him do) and informed me that his close friend's wife had passed away from a heart attack. I asked him if he wanted me to come over, and he said he did. So I left work and went to be with him. Days later, we took him to the funeral, and after, he informed us we didn't need to come over anymore, that he needed to be there for his friend. He was that kind of guy. He could barely get in and out of the car or walk into the grocery store, but he was determined to take care of his friend. Of course, we never listened.

During his last days, he insisted I take him to the western clothing store so he could buy my daughter a shirt. Then, before Father's Day, I was driving him home from the doctor after he told them he wouldn't be back, and he informed me he wanted me to take him one day soon to get my husband a card. He said, "He ain't my father, but he is one hell of a father."

Until his last day, he was thinking of us.

In his last days, we had picnics in his living room and watched the news with him. CNN was his favorite channel.

Days before he took a turn for the worse I sensed it was coming, and so did he. He had a little notebook that recorded what he did each day, what he ate, our visits, and how he felt. I assumed it was his way of remembering details as he sensed his mind slipping. In that book he recorded something about how he had played a good game, and he was done on Wednesday of the following week.

I arrived one June morning toward the end with his favorite Starbucks latte, which he'd decided he'd treat himself to regularly after years of claiming Starbucks was too expensive. We sat on the edge of his front porch, where we could touch the grass with our feet. He wore his slippers, and I had bare feet. On the ride to his house, I thought about how I'd tell him what was in my heart and inform him of the positive impact he'd made in my life. I had to tell him the depths of healing he'd brought to my life. As we brushed at the grass with our feet, we conversed about lighthearted matters. I gathered the courage to be vulnerable while contemplating if he'd shut down or reject what I was determined to tell him. My dad had passed without me telling him how much I loved him and how much I had craved his love and acceptance, but I would not let it happen again.

I swallowed back my nerves. "Jimmy."

"Yeah." He glanced sideways at me.

"I want to tell you something."

He lowered his head as though sensing I had something on my mind. "What's that?"

"You will never know how much you have healed me. You were everything I ever wanted in a father. You accepted me for me, and I am so grateful for your love and acceptance. Thank you for the joy you've brought my family and me."

I can't recall what he said in return, perhaps because I breathed a sigh of relief to have got it out without breaking down, but I remember him swallowing hard and keeping his gaze pinned on the ground.

Wednesday, the date and day he'd written down in his notebook as the last day he'd fight cancer, he slipped into a coma and never came out. After he remained in that state for a few days, I stood at his bedside, lifted his hand, and told him we'd be okay, and he didn't have to fight anymore. Later that night, he slipped away, and with his passing, we lost an earth angel.

He indeed was the most selfless person I've ever met. He made cancer look like a walk in the park when we knew it was anything but. He made me want to be better, and to do better, and to see the world through his eyes. He was the hero every little girl seeks in a father. He was my teacher, and I could never thank him enough in life. He taught me what unconditional love was. At times I fantasized that my father had sent him to help heal the child he could not.

When Jimmy joined our pack, he was no longer a lone wolf. He will forever be the angel who helped me find my wings.

19—THE BIRD WITH A
BROKEN WING

"It is hard to write about my own mother. Whatever I do write, it is my story I am telling, my version of the past. If she were to tell her own story other landscapes would be revealed."
~ Adrienne Rich

The most important lesson I've learned in my relationships is to not put expectations on others and allow people to be who they are. Still, in doing so, some relationships required establishing crucial boundaries. This understanding has helped me tremendously in dealing with my mother.

The effect her words have had on her children is something I address. In my search to find freedom from the bonds that tied me to her and to understand the mother wound within me, I had to examine the whole truth behind the woman I viewed as selfish, entitled, and manipulative. I had to separate my emotions and heal the scars by dismantling the triggers and getting to the source of the woman I deem an energy vampire.

The gaping mother wound is evident in the seven daughters she birthed. My mother is complex, and a relationship with her is the most difficult I've ever encountered. At times, I've considered the peace I'd find in my life if I severed all ties, but when I look at her and what she has become, I'm filled with empathy because I see a lost little girl, still wandering the barren lands in search of the ghost of my grandmother.

For most of my life, I considered my mother my seventh sibling. She bore the title of "mother" but never earned the badge in the sense of the guidance, nurturance, and protection a child requires from a mother. Until my late twenties, I solely blamed my father for the trauma and injustices I attached to my childhood; then I realized the responsibility also rested on my mother. Some of my anger shifted to her as I judged her lack of care and believed she had checked out in life.

We didn't ask to be here, I reasoned when I thought of her. She and Dad made a choice to have seven children. It wasn't our fault. In these musings, I realized I still bore the blame that we had been too much for her. And her claims that she didn't understand birth control, which was why she had so many kids, elevated the impression that I was a mistake, a burden, and unwanted.

I don't recall my mother holding or comforting me, or me ever seeking her attention. I don't remember much of her in my daily life. But I know she was there, in the background and often on the phone for hours upon end. However, I do remember her endeavors to mother. For example, before my fourth sister was born, and when I was the baby of the family, I developed a high fever, and I recall hallucinating while lying between my parents in their bed. And another night, as my mother sat on the edge of the bathtub holding me in the steam and trying to sweat out the fever. She tried to make memories and show love with birthday gifts and homemade cakes. Memories like this bring valuable insight that while it appeared she was incapable of mothering at times, other times she was mentally present. So why did she become the wallpaper in my memories?

I needed answers to my endless questions. Why did most of us girls all feel the same disconnect with her? Why did we seek comfort and support in each other over going to her? What happened to the mother-and-daughter bond, or did one ever exist?

Before my father's death, I found the phone relationship with my mother tolerable and was thankful for the two thousand miles that divided us. However, I'm aware the divide in our beliefs and value system created a more significant wedge than what already existed from childhood. Also, interactions with her because of her conversation choices left me drained and dispirited. When I visited my parents, I witnessed how my adult sisters, who still lived with them, exhibited annoyance, and dismissed our mother. In our childhood, she was very much the type of mother to call for you to wait on her hand and foot, a characteristic that still remains. In visiting my family, I gathered that my sisters' attitudes came from irritation at the servitude I recalled experiencing at home. But still, I considered their behavior unacceptable. She was our mother, and she deserved respect. But it wasn't that cut and dried, which I'd come to understand.

Grief

After arriving at my parents' home to aid in my father's funeral arrangements I recall sitting in their living room, observing my mother's suffering. She sat in her armchair, broken, scared, hurt, and numb. She hugged herself and rocked like a young child trying to self-soothe. Everything in me wanted to take her pain away. I told her not to worry. I would figure everything out. She wasn't alone. And I meant every word and have no regrets about the journey this promise would take me on.

Awareness of how my parents treated me even in my adult years never occurred to me. I stepped up and did what I figured I needed to do. I told my siblings she deserved the time to grieve without worrying about bills. My parents didn't have their affairs in order and were struggling financially for years. There was no money to take care of the funeral or my mother. My siblings helped with the funeral. Afterward, not all could afford to help my mother financially, and some chose not to. My husband and I decided to prepay her rent for six months, help with utilities and other miscellaneous bills for her home, clean up loose ends with my dad's business, set up a savings account for her, and the list goes on. I didn't know how to deal with estates or creditors of the deceased. But again, as was customary for me, I went into "fix everything mode." I did what I could in the week I was there, but eventually I had to return home to educate myself on how to clean up the mess left behind.

Four months afterward, my mother and other family members moved to be closer to me. It would be then, seventeen years after I had left home, that I would come to know my mother and the child within who maneuvered her physical form and shocking behaviors.

As I had done from the moment my father passed, I continued to take a caregiver role with my mother and provided a basic understanding of life. Not because she lacked knowledge, sheltered by her faith. Nor because my father controlled her, because she was one person he couldn't. My mother chose not to step outside of her comfort zone.

The lengths I went to in order to make my mom's life easier taught her that she could drop everything on me. I became the go-to person. She would say "Ask Naomi; she will know" or "Naomi will figure it out." She marched into my house, shoved her mail at me, and got me to open it and figure out any problems. She incessantly talked and worried about every little thing: the weather, the condition of the roads, her tires, a noise in her car, her neighbors, and on and on until you thought you were going mad. But I believed, because she didn't have my father, it was my duty to listen and help. She called and sought advice day after day, only to do it her way in the end, which usually added more significant problems that my older sister and I were left to deal with.

My mother is a pressure speaker. She calls and asks you how your day is before quickly cutting you off to accommodate her agenda and what she needs from you.

Throughout those five to six years, I gave her all my time and energy. I believed I was doing right by her. I handed over tens of thousands of dollars to help without hesitation, until I tuned in to the backhanded remarks and lack of appreciation. Her statement that God put my husband and I where we were in life to take care of her, not because we had earned it, offended me. But as usual, I kept my mouth shut. It festered inside of me as I continued behaving as what I deemed to be a dutiful daughter.

The entitlement and the burden of her nature eventually took their toll on me. I observed how she treated us children and her grandchildren as objects. I think it was at this point that my stress and growing annoyance with her turned to anger. As her daughter, I was used to her treating me like her servant, but I would not allow her to do that to my children. My heart went out to my father during these years as I contemplated how he'd put up with her for so long. I recalled how before he died the roles between my parents had considerably differed from how they had been while I was growing up. He worked, did the dishes, did all the shopping, and it seemed as though my mother did little. During this time in her life, her weight had steadily climbed, bringing awareness that she was struggling emotionally. Around this point, the doctor said she'd had a silent heart attack. She stopped sleeping in a bed and slept upright in a recliner, fearing she'd stop breathing if she lay down. She hasn't slept in a bed in over a decade.

As my oldest sister and I continued to aid our mother, we jumped and ran to her every need and often received little appreciation in return. I observed my mother's behavior and that of my daughter, who was a young teen at the time, and wondered if my mother might have stopped mentally maturing. It made no sense to me why a fifty-six-year-old woman acted like she was half dead and utterly incapable of handling the smallest of details. And why at times she acted downright bratty and lashed out at us like a toddler taking a temper tantrum. Out of the need to fix everything, I had put myself into a position that became mentally and physically draining, and I wanted out!

Our relationship grew more toxic, and she was oblivious because her needs were being met, and I concealed the depths of my anger. I had loved my life before my father died. Afterward, I daydreamed of running away and never coming back. I became furious at him for dying and leaving my mother for us to deal with.

She demanded respect. However, respect is earned, and unfortunately, it's something she never obtained from her children. As obedient daughters, most of us surrendered to her demands for respect and reminders of "I am the mother." Respect is bestowed by her children, but not felt in their hearts. She holds that because she is our mother respect is owed to her, without consideration that her adult children also deserve respect. She fails to understand we are not objects conceived to serve her to the detriment of our own happiness and well-being.

Many times, while talking to her on the phone or visiting in person, I feel like someone has just taken a machine gun and pelted me with bullets. Her statements cut to the very core. I remember a conversation between us in her living room when I questioned why my dad hadn't filed for bankruptcy because there was no way out with the amount of debt they had acquired. She became disgruntled and said, "Once you lose everything, you will understand." On another occasion, she said, "Only when you lose your own husband will you understand what I've gone through." I came to believe she wanted me to suffer as she had. So, I internalized her anger and silenced the pain of her words.

A few weeks after Jimmy's death, the grief had become too much and I reached out to her. I sought comfort from her by letting her know my family and I were hurting. But, again, all her words before and after faded as she said, "How do you think I feel? I've dealt with so much death…" I can't explain how often she's turned a situation about others to herself. Eventually you stop caring because the pain and rejection are too much. You become aware that your life, stress, pain, or problems hold no merit to her. She doesn't listen. Her self-serving addictions and need to unleash her pain are too powerful.

The final straw was when we sat in my living room, and she was upset at two of my siblings who had renounced the faith of our upbringing and had decided to follow what resonated with them. She made a statement about how my father died for a reason because he would be ashamed about what we girls had become. As a daughter, this plucked out my heart. I had given her my all. I had set aside my life for those five to six years to help her thrive, and it wasn't enough. There was no pleasing someone who couldn't see past her misery, pain, and indoctrination.

My sisters are honorable women with morals and values, healthy marriages, and families of their own. At their center, they are kind and have a love and respect for others. Do we all have some things we could change about ourselves? Absolutely. But we are people, not dolls situated on our parents' shelf without a hair out of place and a perfect, fixed smile.

I consider my sisters and I strong women, most with minds of our own. Ironically, my dad sought to raise meek, biblical women of times long retired. A time when women, like children, were to be seen and not heard. Later in life, he appeared to appreciate that we were strong women who took charge of our lives. As for my mother, I understood that day in my living room that my sisters and I would never be enough in her eyes because we don't conform to her box; therefore, we are not valued.

I had become my own oppressor in life. I carried anger at other siblings for not doing their part in helping our mother and lightening my load. I was irritated at family members and friends who visited The Bank of Naomi often. But, above all, I was tired of bellyaching about the injustices I felt. I had to admit to myself that I had done this to myself. I had allowed myself to be used. I had lain down and allowed people to walk all over me, and it was my responsibility to change it. I was tired of the heartache and the pain. I was plain old sick and tired of being tired.

So I closed the "bank" and told the family I would no longer take financial responsibility for our mother. This choice initially caused panic and ruffled some feathers with some family members. Because if I wasn't taking on the financial burden, who would? Others fully supported my need to step away. I also removed myself from the role of caregiver and all the other hats I wore regarding my mother. I snipped my puppet strings, took a step back, and again took the seat of the observer in my life. What had to change? What wasn't working?

I established new boundaries for friends and family because I had come to a point where I wondered whether people genuinely liked me, or liked what I could provide for them. I wanted people to pick me for me. I cringe when I think of the women who came into my life around this time, while I was trying to figure out these new boundaries, because upon meeting them I let them know straight up: don't lie to me, and don't ask for money, and we will be good. I'm happy to report some stuck around.

During these years, my mother informed me of my changes and stated I had become hard. So in a sense I suppose the disconnect probably came across that way, but I was trying to figure out how to change my conditioning: that I had to pay people to love and accept me.

The new stance I took allowed me the time to get a clearer insight into the woman who had birthed me. Why, at times, did she feel she needed to compete with her children? Why did she display jealousy over the bond we sisters shared? Why did she choose the phone as her means of communication instead of a physical connection with everyone in her life? What made my mother tick? She was not a cruel woman. She didn't seek to harm others. Despite her claims that she knew she needed to change, she didn't care to. When I allowed my hurt and emotions to emerge, I processed the remark as a relationship with my sisters, and I wasn't important enough for her to change. However, as I healed, I could view the statement with a clearer perspective. She was aware, but didn't care to because it took work to change. It took courage. And perhaps she didn't feel courageous enough to take on the challenge.

Throughout the healing process, I had to evaluate the files I had kept stored within me titled, "Reasons My Mother Is Unfit and Doesn't Love Me," following the same process I had used with the files I had collected of my father, "The Boogeyman," "The Monster," "My Oppressor." I retrieved my magnifying glass and went to work.

I analyzed the endless questions I had concerning my mother. Why does she gravitate to the horrors happening in the world? Why do these types of topics dominate her conversations? Why does she need to overtalk everyone? Why does she squirm at any sign of emotion? Why does she commandeer her daughters' time and emotions? Why does she care so much what other people think of her or her children? What's with her incessant worrying about everything? And…why is she incapable of being the mother I need her to be?

I sifted through my blocked emotions and the anger I harbored toward her. And in essence, I discovered I wanted her to work harder as a mom—a desire that intensified to outrage when she disregarded my siblings' and my grief over my dad's death and made herself the focus. I don't believe anyone has the right to tell another how they should grieve, but in the circumstance with my mother, I wondered when it had turned from helping a grieving mother and wife to enabling. After the requisite five to six years of grace for her mourning, I refused to enable the victim-mentality trap she had fallen into. I wanted her to stop wallowing in self-pity and to get back up. I wanted her to bloody live! To see the beauty in her life. Not to become consumed with what she didn't have but embrace her thirteen children and sons-in-law and fifteen grandchildren. Yes, Dad was gone. Yes, the pain of losing a spouse, parent, or child is something one can never understand until they go through it, but our loved ones would want us to get back up, even on days when we want to hide from the world. Grief is not easy. And silently, I demanded that she require more of herself.

Try as I might, I couldn't shake my debilitating anger and bitterness toward her. For once in my life, I needed her to be the mother and allow me to be the daughter. I was sick of the servitude mentality my parents had adopted for us. I was sick of being objectified, and I was done with my mother doing it to my sisters, our husbands, and our children. I was sick of her love and acceptance coming with conditions.

Then I met a mentor who told me about the Ho'oponopono mantra, a prayer for forgiveness. I'd never heard of it before, so I looked it up. It originated in Hawaii and was initially taught by Morrnah Nalamaku Simeona.

Again, the simplistic concept seemed so easy I wondered how it could possibly work. I thought, well, what do I have to lose? So I started reciting the mantra in my head before and after phone conversations and during physical interactions with my mother. To my surprise, it worked like magic. I felt calm and went to a place in my mind where my mother's negativity couldn't enter. The mantra gave me a sense of what personal freedom from triggers felt like. It quelled my triggers involving my mother enough to make me want more of that peace in my life.

During the weeks following this new lifeline, I stumbled upon a clip from an old Oprah show that profoundly resonated with me. Oprah spoke of how we have an idea of what our mothers should be or what we want them to be. Her guest, Bishop TD Jakes, said that sometimes our parents are broken when we get them. He spoke of how some of us are voluminous, ten-gallon people born into families of pint-sized capacities. Those words hit me straight in the heart, and I crumpled into a sobbing mess.

I cried for the years I wasted harboring ill feelings toward the parents I thought I deserved and the ones I received.

Simple theories like Bishop Jakes's insight and the Hawaiian prayer propelled me toward healing at a speed greater than I could ever have imagined. I'd never received advice so profound in therapy. As I changed my mindset, I was surprised how quickly outdated emotions and wounds that no longer served me vanished. I felt a great sense of healing and freedom. I learned to accept my mother precisely as she was and that when I expected her to be anything different than what she was, I was causing harm to myself. I loved her, but I didn't have to like her behavior, and I had the right to put healthy boundaries in place to shield myself from her self-imposed prison of negativity, anxiety, and depression.

One night I awoke to the sound of my mother calling my name. My husband lay asleep beside me, and there was no one in my room. I lay there pondering the eerie experience, and something told me I had to go to my mother and apologize for the feelings I had carried for her. The following day, a basket of nerves, I sat outside her apartment and said a quick prayer before going inside. We chatted for a few minutes before I told her I needed to tell her something, and I noted the anxiety in her gaze. I started in with, "I wanted to apologize to you. I've harbored feelings against you—"

And it was then she cut me off. She started babbling something I don't recall, and I held up a hand as tears of panic rose. "Please, please! Just hear me out. It's not bad, I promise." I attempted to calm the anxiety I observed in her. "I wanted you to be the mother I needed you to be. And you weren't, and I accept you gave me what you could. I'm sorry for the feelings I've carried."

I don't recall what else I said, but as I spoke, she squirmed in her seat and appeared to want to jump out of her skin. I realized then she was uncomfortable with emotions, tears, and feelings. Is this why she overtalked people? Was it her way of controlling the conversation to avoid emotions and feelings? If so, why did talking about matters of the heart bother her so much?

She mumbled her own apology and gave me a brief hug at the door as I left. Although I left not receiving the openness I hoped for and had to rush to be heard, I accepted that what I received was all she could give. And I was okay with that.

Trauma's Echoes

As I had processed my healing concerning my father, I looked at my mother as a little child. I took the journey into her childhood and family history to unravel her behaviors and predisposed fears.

My grandfather was a family man and took with him to his grave the secret that he was adopted. He married my grandmother and had two sons, who both died in infancy—one a few days after being born, and the other at nine months. My grandparents went on to have my mother and, a couple years later, my uncle. When my uncle was three or so, my grandmother got cancer, which started in her eye and spread to her breasts. I recall hearing stories of her glass eye.

Throughout my mother's life, my grandmother was in and out of hospitals and heavily medicated. Sometimes she lashed out and said horrible things to my mother and uncle, things a child should never hear from a parent. I can only imagine the guilt and shame my mother dealt with for simply being alive, with the statements spoken to her.

My grandfather had to make a living for the family, and as a truck driver, he was often on the road, leaving my uncle and mom in the care of my great-grandfather and other relatives.

At one point, my grandmother attempted suicide because dealing with cancer and grief in her life had become too much. It would only stand to reason that her attempt to take her own life profoundly impacted her family.

As a child, never knowing when your mother was coming home from the hospital or if at all had to have caused my mother heaps of worry and fear. Also, having multiple caregivers would have added to her insecurities and fear.

Having my grandfather and great-grandfather playing a more dominant role in her life than her mother, I can only assume that she too would've lacked crucial guidance on becoming a woman.

My grandmother died when my mother was sixteen, when a daughter needs her mother more than ever. A year later, my mother married my father, and within a year or so, she had my first sister.

I believe the absence of a secure foundation, nurturance, and guidance from her own mother has left my mother greatly unmothered. How could she give us what she didn't receive? My defense used to be "Well, look what I came from and how I parented my own children." But some people are stronger than other people, some would say. To which I'd grow agitated and say, "Well, I'm tired of always being the strong one."

My healed self realizes that the difference between my mother's parenting and mine is my awareness that I needed to break the cycle and the diligence to see it through, no matter the cost. My mother has kept herself tucked safely inside a cocoon all her life. Like a squirrel hides its acorns, she has stored away her pain, never to emerge.

My mother's brother died two years ago. He never married or had children. I don't recall him ever dating, although I heard stories of him dating one girl, and she broke his heart, and that was it. While I was growing up, he lived at my grandparents' old homestead until he moved into the house my grandfather and step-grandmother shared. He lived with my grandfather for years. After my grandfather passed, he stayed in the house with his half sister, Katie. He never ventured far from home and kept the same job most of his life. He had a set routine and stuck to it day in and day out. He, too, chose to stay within the safety of his cocoon. He was kind, like my grandfather, but horribly shy.

He owned the old homestead of my grandparents, and on his death, Katie brought me my grandmother's old suitcase filled with her trinkets and bits and bobs for my mother because the homestead had become dilapidated and was set to be torn down. Because I'm a lover of history, I asked my mother if I could look through my grandmother's things before bringing the suitcase to her. She said she didn't mind, and honestly, with how my mother operates, she would have probably left the suitcase at my home indefinitely, as she left my father's totes full of belongings for close to eight years before I said we needed to let them go.

I sat on the floor and sorted through my grandmother's belongings. It was as though I had stepped into the past as I held the empty perfume bottles, her pill organizers, various brooches, and the bronze blush compact with the powder in the shade she'd worn still intact. I sensed the tragic tale of a woman I never knew, and yearned to know more of her with each item. I believe

171

she had wanted to be a devoted mother, but heartache, loss, and sickness had sent her down another path. I wondered how many times she lay in her hospital bed, sick and in pain, longing for her two children at home, and the comfort they would bring if she could hold them in her arms and breathe in the scent of their love and innocence. Or the support and comfort she would find in my grandfather's arms. How many times had she cried herself to sleep?

Then I thought of my mother and how many times she fell asleep at night, scared and longing for the safety of my grandmother's embrace.

I thought of my grandfather making the long, lonely trips driving a truck to put food on the table. And how many days and nights he worried and stressed about whether that would be the day his wife passed. Or how his children were faring without them both.

In the suitcase, I came across a letter my mother had written to her mother. My heart fractured at the opening of "Dear Mama," written in my mother's beautiful handwriting. My mother was younger when writing the letter, and she wanted to go to a birthday party but didn't have a gift, and was writing her mother in the hospital, asking how she was going to get one. I contemplated how many times their communication had to be through letters. I grieved for the child in the letter. I grieved for my adult mother, my uncle, and my grandparents.

It was as though my grandmother had stepped through time to ensure the suitcase was delivered to me. Those moments, sitting and getting to know the ghost of my grandmother, are a gift I'll treasure forever. It helped me understand my mother and the little girl inside of her that still feels abandoned, scared, vulnerable, and lonely.

Grace

My mother doesn't have strong connections in her life and doesn't put much effort into people. So instead, she uses the phone as her means of contact. Not long ago, she admitted she'd rather talk on the phone than visit in person. I used to get irritated over her lack of care and her addiction to the phone until I connected the dots. The phone isolates her from the world, which I don't believe she wants but it's a barrier she puts up to keep people out. If you don't let people too close or form bonds, you minimize the risk of getting hurt.

Another nuisance we girls have experienced when it comes to our mother is her need to call to constantly remind you of everyone's birthdays, anniversaries, anniversaries of their death, etc. We have a huge family, so there are many special days to celebrate in the run of a year, and she is like Siri on speed dial. She remembers everything like an elephant. I asked her what time I was born, and she rambled off a time. And recently, while moving, I stumbled across a canvas she had made with the time, date, and other birth details about me. She had remembered to the minute when I'd been born. It amazed me. I'm sure many mothers remember the time of their child's birth, but I only have two children, and I know the hour they were born, but not the minute. When I found the canvas, I called her to let her know she had been right. And what she said to me provided further insight into how she looked at life. She said, "I don't want to forget anything. It's the way I've always been." But of course she didn't want to forget! The memories she had created with her own mother were few, and because of it, she seized every important date and time, attempting to not forget. As she had probably clung to every detail of her mother's face with each encounter, trying to seal the memory of my grandmother into her mind, lest she forget.

Forgiveness is for us. It doesn't make what happened to us okay. Some atrocities children have faced at the hands of their parents go far beyond what I ever experienced. Forgiveness is you reclaiming your life and stepping into your personal power.

In setting aside my own pain and realizing my mother's behaviors had nothing to do with me and all to do with her; I could heal my scars. I realized my mother had never been consistent in her parenting, and as a child, I'd never trusted her. She wasn't my safe place to fall. She had no clue how to mother, and I no longer blame her for her shortcomings. She did the best she knew how, and unfortunately for us girls, with her awareness of the pain she has caused, she has chosen not to change. I don't believe it comes from a place of selfishness and lack of love, but out of fear of what pain she will face when filtering through the past. It takes courage to heal, and I wish, with everything in me, she'd find the courage. However, I accept that she may never find healing. And if she did, I suspect her indoctrination would keep her from embracing her daughters for what they are and without conditions. If she could only see the gifts granted her, she wouldn't have to walk her life alone.

I witness the mother wound in my sisters and the yearning for acceptance and support from our mother, which keeps a child trapped.

If my sisters and mom let go of the secrets, the shame, and the guilt, a beautiful sisterhood could emerge.

Food for Thought

When I started viewing my mother as a person without the conditions of what I thought a mother should be, and stopped judging her for her unwillingness to change, her oppressive opinions no longer seized my thoughts or triggered me.

I learned to stand firm in my truth by releasing the slavish bondage I had to my parents. Healthy bonds are essential, especially with family.

Philosopher and advocate of women's rights, Mary Wollstonecraft, stated, "A slavish bondage to parents cramps every faculty of the mind."

Too often, children grow up thinking they owe their parents because they created them. Therefore, we form a relationship of bondage with them. As a result, we often give them a pass on all their deficiencies. We adopt the mentality that we must shut up, take it, and allow them to make us feel small and inadequate and place their needs above our own.

We have the right to choose who and how much we allow others into our lives. We are no longer children. We get to choose who plays in our sandbox. We must value ourselves enough to respectfully assert our opinions and feelings to our parents, particularly when they are violating our boundaries. Our silent vow of loyalty to family and parents can sometimes silence us from doing what is best for ourselves. If we question or oppose our parents' views, it doesn't mean we don't respect or love them. It simply means we are an adult with our own thoughts and feelings. Our parents' beliefs and opinions shouldn't become our law. How many times have we protected their feelings and relinquished our own? Each time we fear our parents' reactions or silence our truth to protect them, we reject ourselves. Enough with the secrets. We aren't responsible for their happiness. It's not about condoning the wrongs people have done to us, it's about taking our power back. Guilt, shame, and blame are powerless acts.

As we peel back the layers of trauma, we unravel more we need to work on. So, you may wonder, why would I even bother healing if it takes so much effort? Because with the release of every emotion and pain stored within your mind and body comes liberation, and with it, every ounce of pain you experience is worth the reward.

No matter how much I've healed, my mother sometimes pushes me to the point of insanity. In the last year, I dealt with a situation with my mother that left me shaken and feeling like the little girl that I'd spent years convincing that it was safe to step into the light and be seen. A conflict had arisen in the family over my uncle's death, and I wanted no part of it. My mother called me as I was lying in bed one night. She had been pushing the issue and wanting to talk about it. And despite my telling her multiple times during the conversation to leave me out of it, she wouldn't stop talking about it. Each time I would remind her, her voice would rise, and she became aggressive in her need for me to take her side. And as I started to feel backed into the corner, unheard and disrespected, I jumped out of bed. I wasn't going to permit her to bully me into hearing what she had to say. She had overstepped her boundaries and disrespected me. I quickly told her I was sorry, but I had to hang up now. And I did exactly that. It didn't feel good because we were trained to respect our parents. After all, they are our elders. It upset me to hang up on her because I believe in people's right to be heard, but I can no longer allow mistreatment when it comes to my personal well-being, mother or not.

After the conversation, I ran a bath. I sat in the tub, hugging my knees, shaking, and crying out of frustration. Why couldn't she respect my choice not to engage in the conversation? Why doesn't she ever listen? Why had she forced me to feel backed into the corner, so I had no choice but to hang up? My choice to end the call wasn't easy, but I did it for myself. I deserve to be respected and treated justly. That choice caused my mother not to speak to me for two months, and honestly, it was a peaceful two months. I've become familiar with the naughty stool she likes to put her adult daughters on, but it no longer affects me.

Ho'oponopono Prayer

I'm sorry. Please forgive me. Thank you. I love you.

Affirmation

I accept the parents I cannot change. I allow others to be who they are. I am deserving of respect, acceptance, and love. Love comes freely to me.

20–THE LITTLE WOMEN

"Siblings—the definition that comprises love, strife, competition and forever friends." ~ **Byron Pulsifer**

My sisters and I have grumbled, over the years, about why our parents had so many kids, and at times I considered which ones I'd give back. But thankfully, there was a no refund policy, because each of them brings quality to my life in her own way.

My role as mother and sibling to my sisters caused confusion and blurred the boundaries of our relationships. However, an endearing memory I have involves my baby sister soon after I left home. Although I no longer lived at home I still attended the church and would see my family there, but usually at a distance. My parents didn't approach me, and I dodged them because I was afraid to see the disappointment in their eyes and scared of being dragged back home. But one Sunday morning after service, I stood with my boyfriend and now-husband in the churchyard, and my youngest sister called out my name. And I remember quickly looking over her head for my parents, half expecting them to swoop in and snatch her away.

Nevertheless, she raced toward me, her face and eyes

aglow with delight to see me. She stopped and peered up at me, her beautiful brown doe eyes filled with admiration and esteem before she looked me over from head to toe and said, "You look beautiful today." Then she handed me a note she had written to me, which I have kept all these years. Her kindness and unconditional love hugged my heart. I recall thinking that she still loved me, despite my abandoning her, and gratitude welled in my eyes.

I'd worn a new black skirt with large red roses and a black button-up silk top that day...

After I moved to the other side of Canada, the separation and time created a break between my little sisters and us. They were the sisters I felt closest to, yet I never thought I belonged with them because of the age gap. However, I never fit in with my two oldest, either. I never felt a connection to my oldest sister because she was more like a parent than a sibling. She was exactly what my parents had wanted in a daughter. She was the first to report to them about your misdeeds. She was also obedient, righteous, and responsible. Because she was the oldest and came with what my parents considered admirable qualities, they nominated her as the third parent. She would hold this favored position in their eyes until she stepped out of line and left the faith. Only when she broke through the rigidness of our conditioning could she and I start to form a relationship.

My second-oldest sister and I were fifteen months apart, and I assume because of the small gap between our births, my mother often bought us the same things, only in different colors. She had the smarts but learned to lie and manipulate at a young age. She batted her lashes at my dad and swayed her hips to get her way, and it used to agitate me. And I judged her for it, often chiming in my head that over my dead body would I ever stoop so low. I'm sure my dad's sights turned on me for this reason.

She was a regular little thief as a kid. Back when one of the back rooms of our farmhouse doubled as a church, she stole the money from the offerings and shared it with me. We had pink and teal backpacks and were on our way out the front door for school with plans for what we would purchase at the school canteen when my mother heard the change rattling in our packs. Another time I recall her emptying my parents' old glass milk jar of change. I don't think she shared it with me, though. Maybe it was then that my dislike for her started, or the multiple times my parents believed her over me. I received my share of spankings over her lies. She is the one sister I remember getting into a hair-pulling fight with.

She was also the one who got to do the grand march the year before me and the one the teachers compared me to. She was also the one the boys liked first. So I would say there was some rivalry there, too. However, by her final year at home, she and Mom fought rings around each other, and my parents decided it was time for her to leave. They sent her thousands of miles away.

Around this time, my dad suggested I would be next. He said he'd arrange a marriage for me. Most likely, he was trying to get me worked up, but from experience, I didn't put it past him that he may do just that. After all, our lives were straight out of the 1800s. Again I thought, over my dead body would he choose my husband for me. I believe the fire simmering inside me helped me keep my sanity in the prohibitive existence under my father's roof.

Regarding my second-oldest sister, I remember her

calling home sometime after she had been living on her own, my mom getting on her back, and me jumping to her defense. Our relationship wasn't the best for decades, but she has become one of my most incredible supporters in our later years. And honestly, family matters the most to her. I love that about her.

The separation between my younger sisters and I lengthened with my absence, and I remember returning to my hometown to get married and seeing my little sisters for the first time. My second-youngest sister, who always had a skip to her step, bounced toward me with eagerness and delight to see me. I recall being taken aback at how much she had changed. She had grown-up and stood eye to eye with me. She had held me in as a fond memory as I had them, but I hadn't changed much to her. For me, the little girls I had left behind had grown into little women. Love swelled in my heart at the glee on her face and the faces of those who followed her.

The memory that stands out as nearest and dearest to my heart with my two older sisters is our reenactments of the 1949 version of *Little Women* starring June Allyson, who played Jo March. This version of *Little Women* will forever be my favorite. Initially, I was assigned the role of Jo because I was very much the tomboy. I adored June's deep voice, and I loved the character Louisa May Alcott created in Jo because she had a mind of her own and wouldn't be confined by society's perception of what women should be. She also had spunk. My oldest sister had the role of Meg, and she effortlessly mirrored Janet Leigh's mannerisms. We girls used to refer to our oldest sister as prim and proper because she acted much older than her age and mirrored Anne of Green Gables, with the same up-do and all in her daily life. She also had the fixed jaw of Megan Follows in the 1985 Canadian television series.

My second-oldest sister was Beth, and she also easily adapted to Margaret O'Brien's mannerisms as Beth. In fact, she looked as though she and Margaret could be sisters. So that leaves us with Amy, the stunning Elizabeth Taylor, who also played her role brilliantly. My sisters also gave me her part, which I had to adapt to because I found her character spoiled and entitled, but eventually she grew on me, and I became intrigued with her.

I took my parts seriously and studied the characters and their mannerisms. I watched and rewound the VHS over and over. I suppose observing characters and other people came naturally to me.

I loved the March sisters' friendship, which mirrored the camaraderie I shared with my sisters in our childhood, and now. Children are adaptable and brilliant little humans, and to live forever in the mind of a child could be quite liberating. We girls found a way to live and thrive outside the confines of the homestead and our parents' restrictions.

As much as my sisters were the joy in my childhood, they were also a pain in the backside. I started dating my husband in secret when I was seventeen. Dating in my upbringing was very different from what society would consider dating. I only saw my future husband when we made the hour-long drive to church on Sundays and Wednesdays. I looked forward to each service because not only would I see him, but friends as well. He wrote me letters, and I got all mushy inside as I scrolled over the sweet nothings he had written. I hid my secret under my mattress. Honestly, what was it with me hiding things under the mattress? You would have thought, by seventeen, I'd have wised up and found a more efficient place to hide something. However, the hiding place had been a safe spot until it wasn't. I don't remember the culprit, but one of my younger sisters found the letters and raced through the house with them in hand. My heart dropped, but I managed to get the letters back and don't remember anything coming from it.

When my oldest sister got her driver's license and my parents were away for extended vacations, she drove us to borrow movies and video games from one of my friends at school. Some of my cherished memories are these times, when my sisters and I cozied up on the couch while others gathered on the floor with blankets to spend hours watching *Dr. Quinn, Medicine Woman*, newer versions of *Little Women* and *Anne of Green Gables*, or to play Mario Bros. Then, as my parents' return neared, we gathered up the games and videos and returned them to remove all evidence.

The support system my siblings and I have forged as adults is invaluable. We are each unique and bring something valuable to our relationships. The commonality of our story gave us a foundation to build trust, acceptance, and sisterhood like none other. We can say what we want about the other but, be warned, don't let an outsider try. We have not always seen eye to eye, and we don't need to. However, with maturity, some of us have learned to agree to disagree, while others…well…that is their story to tell.

My sisters are a blessing to my life and the light in a bleak childhood. For this, I will be forever grateful to my mother for what it took to go through pregnancy and labor seven times. That is a triumph. I don't think I could have done it. So, well done, Mom!

As for my dad, his task wasn't so laborious as to bring seven children into the world, but I credit him for putting up with a house of eight women, which translates to tons of emotions. Perhaps that is why he always escaped to the woods or out of town on business. I had one daughter, and let me tell ya, she was a blessing and a chore. The man should have earned a medal. I'm beyond grateful for all the times he got up for work when perhaps he was too weary but did what was required to raise his family. I'm thankful that he did his best to put food on the table and a roof over our heads. My parents weren't perfect, but who is?

Did I bear the scars of their transgressions? Sure. But it was in the lessons of these experiences that I became who I am today. They also gave me the greatest blessings in the women who have become my most incredible friends. So, to my parents, I've extended grace and forgiveness.

Sisterhood

We all seek to belong and be part of a community. When my family could not be what I needed due to the miles between us and the wedge formed earlier on, I found acceptance and value in several amazing female friends. They opened their lives and families to allow me to be part of their family traditions. I observed their interactions with their families, and in some resonated with their dysfunctions, while in others I yearned for the relationships they shared with their moms. Also, I cultivated what relationships I wanted with my own children as adults.

These women filled the void of family and helped me see the value in friendships and sisterhood. As women, we often feel a need to compete when we should be lifting each other up. We each bring meaning to the world. When we understand there is enough success, love, and money for us all, we release all struggles, and life flows naturally.

Affirmations

Life is good. I choose to acknowledge my blessings. The past no longer has a hold on me.

21–EMPATHY

"Learning to stand in somebody else's shoes, to see through their eyes, that's how peace begins. And it's up to you to make that happen. Empathy is a quality of character that can change the world." ~ **Barack Obama**

"You never really understand a person until you consider things from his point of view—until you climb into his skin and walk around in it." ~ **Harper Lee, *To Kill a Mockingbird***

Many situations in life make for impactful moments and offer opportunities to learn, but it's what we choose to do with the experiences that counts.

The discrimination and ostracization I faced in my youth for being different, and as a woman, formed my habit of observing the happenings in the world around me and striving to understand others and their struggles.

We are so quick to judge without learning the complete story. Some lose their way and wander in life, and society writes them off, considering them worthless. But if we stop to understand and hear their stories, we would be amazed at what unravels. What is the story behind the empty eyes of the homeless person on the street? Do they suffer from mental illness? Are they a veteran who fought for our country? Perhaps they became addicted to drugs and alcohol as a way of suppressing an abusive home life. What of the person who believes their only value in life is to sell their body? Or the kid regarded as a disruption to the rest of the class. What has, or is, happening in their lives? Maybe they never received a hand up or the support they needed to heal. One life is as valuable as the next, and we all deserve to be heard and seen. Each of us is a box of crayons, coloring different pictures in the world. We must value all, including the broken, because these crayons draw the most magnificent pictures and disclose impactful insights into change in a world significantly in need of healing.

Angel Behind the Curtain

At twenty, I became pregnant with my son. He was a high-risk pregnancy and I had to go for frequent ultrasounds after my third month of pregnancy. The whole process of the pregnancy with him was traumatic. At one point after an ultrasound, a doctor took my husband and I into a room and told us our son could be born with serval birth defects. I panicked as the possible defects were listed, and left the appointment scared, but determined to bring my son into the world regardless.

I remember how alone I felt during my pregnancy. I lived in a new city and had no friends. My husband worked a lot, and often went out of town for work. I didn't have a car and would stay holed up in our apartment for weeks on end. The relationship between my parents and me was still fractured at this point, and turning to them for comfort didn't appeal to me. It was a dark time in my life, and I remember crying a lot. I purchased a red notebook and titled each entry "Dear Baby." I poured my love for my unborn child into those pages, and at times released my pain too. Writing in the baby journal gave me comfort.

I received all my education about pregnancy from a birthing book I had purchased and read from cover to cover to make sure I didn't miss anything. I was excited to see my child but terrified of the delivery. At an ultrasound, the doctor came into the room after the nurse went to fetch him. One quick look at the screen, and he swore and said my son needed to come out that day because there was no amniotic fluid left. Unfortunately, my husband was out of town working, and I called him to let him know.

I checked into the hospital a few hours later and started the process of inducing labor, which came with every option they had and four days of pain, weariness, and worry. My son would be born premature, and I wasn't sure what deformities he might have.

The last night in the hospital, before my son finally decided to enter the world, I was placed in a room with another young woman. Earlier, when the nurse had shown her to her bed, I got a glimpse of her through the gap in the curtain, enough to see she was of Indigenous descent.

All day she remained at one centimeter dilated. We never spoke or saw each other face to face. But as the lights went down that night, I lay there listening to her weeping. I wondered if it was from the pain or something more. Finally, I decided to ask her if she was okay, and as we opened to each other, she let me know her child had been conceived out of gang rape. I froze at her revelation and didn't know how to respond. What does one say to another who has faced atrocities beyond anything you can ever imagine? The injustice she had endured fueled the passion in me for the wrongs imposed on others. Also, a keen sense of admiration rose for the strength and courage she had to bring a child into the world that had been conceived out of such pain and tragedy.

Throughout the night, we chatted, drawing comfort from each other. Unfortunately we were taken to delivery rooms the next day as our labor progressed, and I never saw her again.

I've often thought of her throughout the years and wondered what became of her. Did she keep her baby or give it up? Had she healed from her trauma?

Last spring I visited Vancouver Island, searching for my next home, and saw red dresses hanging from trees. They were part of the REDress Project and represented all of Canada's missing or murdered Indigenous women and girls. My soul was heavy, thinking of the suffering of these women, girls, and their families. My mind went to the young woman in the hospital, and the horrors inflicted on her. What had become of her? Had she, too, become a statistic?

I reflected on the night I shared with her and how our different ethnicities never divided us, as it often does in today's society. We were simply two frightened women from different ways of life, each with our own traumas, and about to be new mothers. We found support and comfort in each other. She needed me that night, and I needed her.

She will forever be my angel behind the curtain.

The Gentle Giant

I remember the darkness of his skin, glowing like a beautiful evening sky, and the way he ducked to get through the door. But most of all, I recall the brilliant smile that spread from ear to ear as he looked at me standing by the side of the couch. He saw me, and I saw him.

The gentleman had come to hunt at my father's hunting resort, and I've never forgotten his smile or kindness toward me.

A situation during his stay remained with me throughout my life. I would have been around ten at the time. I remember standing again in the living room as he dipped through the outside door, just as a short white man went to step out. The white man spat on him and remarked that he had no right to walk through the door simultaneously with him. I didn't understand what was happening and, frightened by the man's aggression, I pushed back against the wall. As the incident unfolded, I became aware that there was something about the Black man's skin the other man didn't like.

Afterward, I recall the heated voices of the white man and my father outside.

The Black man wore a navy-blue shirt that day…

The Child Within

My paternal grandmother was a stoic woman on the surface, and it was the only side of her I ever witnessed. In my and my sisters' experience, she wasn't the affectionate type who would shower us with love and kindness, or take note of our birthdays. I considered her prim and proper, a woman to whom I applied the title "grandmother" but with no emotions attached.

My dad's funeral was the first time I had seen her in twenty years. I observed the way she sat, with her emotions concealed, and how her behavior differed from the grief of my mother and siblings, expressed in their body language and faces. Yet I never questioned my grandmother or her ability to keep it together, and only later learned how strong this woman was to deal with life's challenges. At the reception, I noticed my grandmother sitting in a chair and my husband kneeling beside her, compassion and tenderness on his face. I don't know what words passed between them, but the look on my grandmother's face gave me pause. She sat leaning forward and holding his hands. The habitual veil of strength had lowered, and she eyed him, a man she had only met once, with a keen look of respect and vulnerability. I wondered what had passed between them for her to lower her guard enough to look at him so.

I turned back to speak to the family members and friends who had come to support us, and when I looked back some time later, my husband had settled at my grandmother's feet while she continued to talk. Later, when I questioned him about what had transpired between them, he told me he had approached her to offer his condolences, and perhaps she'd sensed his high sensitivity to others and deemed him a safe person with whom to communicate her grief—she opened to him. As she spoke, he knelt beside her and allowed her to talk while he listened. My love for my husband only grew that day because of the kindness and compassion he'd given my grandmother.

Over the following days, the family went out for supper, and my grandmother ambled in with my grandfather. She seated herself at the end of the table, next to me. But when she looked down the table and saw my husband, she excused herself and scooted her eighty-five-year-old self from the booth, saying she was going to talk with "that young man." She never knew he was my husband because she didn't know which granddaughter I was. She knew I was one of the seven. However, instead of being offended that my husband had caught my grandmother's eye, I found amusement in her speedy shuffle to get to him. And in the time or two we visited her in the next couple of years, he continued to draw her attention. On occasion, she'd relate how kind he was—and handsome, too, she'd add. I liked this side of my grandmother. But despite these brief connections, I never pursued building a relationship with her.

My grandparents decided to return to their hometown, with the desire to live the rest of their days there. But, unfortunately, my grandmother had developed dementia before doctors diagnosed my grandfather with brain cancer. After his death, her disease had progressed so far that my aunts decided to place her in a nursing home.

When my mother's brother passed, I returned to my hometown for his funeral. However, the urgency to visit my grandmother plagued me because I figured she didn't have much time left.

I had never been around people with dementia, and nursing homes made me nervous because of an experience visiting my great-grandmother in a home as a child. I recall the screaming and crying of some patients and another throwing a chair into the hallway, all of which terrified me. Still, I was determined to give my grandmother my time and release any harbored emotions inside of me for a woman I believed never cared for my father's children.

My sister, who lived nearby and visited our grandmother often, took me to see her twice in the three days I was there. And the firm and unaffectionate grandmother I remembered had disappeared entirely, replaced with a sweet, loving, fragile woman. My sister introduced me to her as her granddaughter. She eyed me with wonder, looking at me fully with admiration and delight that I belonged to her. She wanted to know everything about me, and I told her whatever she wanted to know.

"Who are you, dear?" she asked one minute later, a smile of confusion on her thin lips.

"I'm Naomi. Your granddaughter."

"Oh." She brightened. "Who are your parents?"

I named my parents.

She nodded as recognition struck her. "Isn't that something. Where is Amos?" she asked of my father, her son. Again, confusion and worry shone in her eyes. "I had six children. I think one of them died. But I don't know how…" Her voice drifted off.

I quickly concealed my shock at her reference to my father. I had no experience to relate her behavior to, but I quickly grasped that this was the disease as she broke her trance and looked at me. "Who are you, dear?" She regarded me with the innocence of a child.

Her vulnerability broke my heart, and I softened to her. Gone was the stoic woman who came with boundaries erected by herself, by my mother, and later by me; in her place sat a defenseless woman at the end of her life. Her time on earth was ending, and I had never truly known her. To protect myself, I had dismissed her as a grandmother because of conditioned beliefs.

Affirmation

I see each person as valuable. Therefore, I am doing my part to understand others the way I want to be understood.

22-UNCONDITIONAL LOVE

"The beginning of love is letting those we love to be perfectly themselves, and not twist them to fit our own image. Otherwise, we love only the reflection of ourselves we find in them." ~ **Thomas Meton, *No Man Is an Island***

You hear people speak of hitting rock bottom, and despite my ups and downs in life, I had never considered obstacles I'd faced as my bottom. But life had more to communicate to me and delivered the lesson at the hand of my daughter. The experience took me to my knees. It was the lowest point in my life, where I had no place to go but up. I had to walk through the valley of grave pain, and it was here where my life took on a whole new meaning. It was here a profound change took place in my life.

History would repeat itself in my daughter and her sudden need to be free from a home life she considered restricting. I saw it coming after she started dating a boy who had more freedoms than her. She started dating him at thirteen, and like most things in her life, she kept their relationship secret from us because she knew we'd disapprove. He wasn't a bad kid, but I had formed an opinion of him early on because of his surface respect to my husband and I and texts I read stating otherwise.

During her relationship with him, she and I had lots of battles. I didn't trust any boy with my daughter, and if I had my way, she wouldn't have dated until she healed the part of herself she had become an expert at suppressing. I also didn't trust her to take care of herself. Although I was aware that my "no dating until sixteen" rule wasn't realistic, I had given it much consideration. If my son, who has always been mature beyond his years, had come to me before the age of sixteen and told me he wanted to date, I would've reconsidered. However, I had an iron hold on my daughter because I feared she didn't value herself enough. And her boyfriend's mother added to my concern. She had no issues with a thirteen-year-old and a fourteen-year-old having sex. Her son was an only child, and the relationship between him and his mom appeared to be more one of friends than of parent and child. Throughout my daughter's teen years, she considered me the uncool parent compared to her friends' parents. Often her comments hurt, and part of me yearned for her acceptance. At times I considered how much easier it would be to just be the friend and not the parent, but my love and concern over her well-being overrode the need for her approval. After all, I was the adult with more life experience.

I suggested to the mother of the boy that we meet. At our meeting I told her how I parented, and I expected her to respect it. I familiarized her with my daughter's struggles to see worth in herself and my fear of her allowing boys to use her body. I also said that I didn't want her to become pregnant before she was ready because she had her whole life ahead of her. Then the mom suggested she could leave condoms around to make me feel better, and during the conversation, she let me know how she was beyond excited to have a grandchild. To be honest, she freaked me out, and I left that conversation with a fixed impression of her. In my mind, her child would never be part of my family.

The boyfriend disliked my husband and I during the four and a half years they dated. I can't say I blamed him. We treated him with kindness, but he knew from conversations with my daughter that we didn't accept him and probably never would. Also, she related to him how unfair she felt the rules we'd set for her were, which is a death sentence to most teens. And by restricting her, we limited their relationship. She pulled away from us during those years, making him her whole world, which is natural for teen relationships. However, bothered at the separation between her and us, I blamed his mother and him for alienating her. Because of my worry over losing a relationship with my daughter, I sat her down multiple times to remind her that sometimes families and people place wedges between each other that can take years to fix. I sensed a tug-of-war between the other mom and me. She wanted to secure a wife for her son, and I wanted to have a healthy relationship with my daughter and raise a woman who stood in her power and understood her worth. But how could I guide her to be what was still lacking in me?

Multiple times I told my daughter that when she was ready to have sex to come to me to discuss it, which never happened because, again, she feared my rejection. I never expected her to wait until marriage like I'd been taught because I didn't believe it was a practical notion. However, my known fear over her not knowing her worth confirmed her silence.

Raising children is hard. We don't always know how to deal with situations that arise, and it's not like the doctor hands you your infant and says, "Oh, by the way, here is the handbook that you will need when little Benny does a, b, or c." No, we are winging this parenting thing, but hopefully with the mindset to learn from our parents' blunders and do better. Maya Angelou said it best when she said, "Do the best you can until you know better. Then when you know better, do better."

I made mistakes in raising my daughter, but I did what I thought was best. With the hurt she went through in school, I would take her on shopping sprees which friends and I called retail therapy in hopes of lifting her spirits. Or we went for lunch and a movie. We chatted and locked fingers on the drive. I affirmed all the fantastic things about her and what she had to offer the world. When I wasn't setting guidelines, in my eyes, our relationship was close.

But in my efforts to take away her pain I spoiled her, and my son resented her for it. She deemed him the golden child in my husband's and my eyes. My son considered her spoiled and commented on the favoritism because she got everything handed to her and he had to work hard for all he got. And they are both valid in their feelings.

Somewhere in life, my daughter learned to be deceitful and became an expert at manipulating my emotions. At times she tried my patience. She was the type of kid who had to have the last say. She had a fire inside her, a defensiveness, and simmering anger she often unleashed on her family. In this regard, she was a walking image of me at her age. But I had been groomed to shield my emotions.

I often felt like I wanted to scream and throw a temper tantrum because she pushed me to my limits. And sometimes I did shout. I recall one day she sat on the floor folding laundry and stated her opinion with determination that she would be heard whether I liked it or not. She had me in such a spin, I didn't know what to think or say because my mind was rotating a million miles an hour. Make sure you don't say anything you can't take back. Frustrated, I finally blurted out, with a stomp of my foot, "I hope you have a daughter ten times as difficult as you." No sooner had I said the words than I regretted them, but instead of fixing it I walked away until I gathered my senses. Later I returned and explained that I didn't want that for her and owned my poor choice of words. But, good god, I felt every one of them in the heat of the moment!

Six months before she graduated, I noticed she had put on a few pounds, and her usual clear complexion had broken out in acne. She also appeared stressed. I questioned her on it, and she brushed it off. My husband and I were set to go to Hawaii to celebrate our anniversary, and she asked if she could come too. Sensing her struggle and that something wasn't right with her, I figured time away from her boyfriend and a change of scenery may help. I talked to my husband, and he agreed but said he wouldn't let her ruin it for us. All vacations leading up to that one had resulted in us dragging a grumbling, miserable teenager around with us. But the trip to Maui ended up being the best time we had had with her in years. We teased her every day, saying, "Guess what?" She replied, already knowing what was coming, "What?" "We love you!" my husband and I would chorus in unison. She would giggle, and you could see her absorb our love. We returned home, renewed and hoping we had strengthened our fractured bond with her, but nothing changed.

When her boyfriend was at our house, I heard her make comments to him, and I questioned her on what I believed were unkind words. Over the years, I had felt bullied by her and didn't like what I saw in her behavior.

But I would learn her behavior came from what was happening behind the scenes with her boyfriend. She told me later that she didn't want to tell me because she didn't want me to say "I told you so." The exact words she had said when she had whined for years about not having her menstrual cycle yet, and I had told her repeatedly, trust me, it's one thing you don't want.

I smile when I recall the day she sat in the passenger seat, and we were driving somewhere, and she looked miserable, but it was not the usual moodiness. I asked her what was wrong, and she said, "I don't want to tell you."

I pressed her further, and she let me know it was her time of the month, and she felt miserable, and how much she hated it. Aware she feared my saying I told you so, something I had never told her in her life, I said, "Yeah, it sucks." Well, in my head I said, *I warned you*. When we are children, all we want to do is grow up, and when we are adults, all we want is the freedom of a kid.

Later it was brought to my attention by a friend that my daughter's boyfriend belittled her and told her she wasn't good for anything but sex. Of course I went into mama bear mode. I discussed it with her, and she covered up for him. The urgency I felt for her to see her worth was at the forefront of the conversation, mixed with my annoyance that she couldn't see herself as I saw her. I projected on her what I saw in myself—my lack of self-worth. Although my upbringing had kept me confined to being a "proper lady," I had always put others before myself.

My perpetual chatter to get through to her came with the insistence that she deserved better than him. Which, of course, didn't go the way I anticipated, but it never had before because she loved him and couldn't see past it. She blamed his mistreatment of her on our restrictions, and on herself for not being good enough.

One afternoon while working in my home office, she came to me and asked me if I had ever experienced sleep paralysis, and

I told her I hadn't. Not sure of what it was, I looked it up while she told me her experiences. I equated them with episodes one of my younger sisters had experienced.

I realized my daughter wasn't sleeping at night when I noticed an empty box of sleeping pills and Tylenol in her trash can. I questioned her on it, but she dismissed it.

A few weeks before her graduation, I was sitting alone in the living room, and she came and sat down beside me. Again stressed and appearing to have been crying, she divulged more than she ever had during her relationship. She informed me she couldn't handle her boyfriend's jealousy and derogatory comments. She revealed they had been fighting more, and she had decided to break up with him.

Our relationship took a turn for the better. She started to glow again, and the weight and acne seemed to vanish overnight. We spent more time on mother-and-daughter dates. Over the following six to eight weeks, my husband and I noticed a positive change in her. She swore off boys, enrolled in college, and showed that she was taking charge of her life. I believed we were over the struggles with her, and the future glowed with promise.

Then she came home from work and told me of a new boy who had started there. I reminded her of her goal and promise to put herself first and not to date for a while. She said, "Yes, I know." But I saw the look in her eyes. The boy made her feel alive. Then one day, she called me from work and told me she wanted to go to his house after work. I became annoyed at her and reminded her again of her promise to herself and us that she would put herself first. At almost eighteen, she should have had more freedom, but I couldn't release my hold out of fear. With contemplation, I decided if there was no way around it, and she would date him, I wouldn't make the mistakes I had before. I had to allow him into our lives and welcome him without judgment. My daughter arranged for him, her, and I to go out for lunch. She let him know he had to pass "the mom test." And upon meeting him, I liked him instantly. He looked me in the eyes and was respectful. I left the lunch impressed and again, feeling perhaps it wasn't bad for them to date.

A week or so later, her work was hosting an after-work BBQ, and she attended, but as the hours ticked by and midnight drew near, I called her to see where she was. I was the type of mother who couldn't sleep until all my little duckies were under my roof. She never answered, and I tried another few times before she finally answered half an hour later. I berated her for being past her curfew and not calling to let us know she would be late. And her response alerted me that something had changed. She came home, and the following morning, I sat her down and asked her why she hadn't called and had talked to me the way she had.

She informed me of all the things I was doing wrong and the injustices she endured at home. The same song and dance we had experienced since she had turned thirteen. That day, instead of fighting her need to be her own boss, I said, "Fine. I think you need to be on your own. I don't know what else to do. When you turn of legal age to get an apartment, your father and I will help you get settled. Between now and then, do what you want to do." I released my hold and had no desire to return to the battle that had transpired for the last five years. She had to learn about life, and I decided I couldn't save her from whatever heartaches may come. I stood up and walked to the fridge to get a glass of water, and she walked upstairs and soon came back with a bag packed.

I asked her where she was going.

She looked at me with a flicker of agitation. "Leaving."

"For where?" I asked.

"You told me to get out. So I'm leaving."

Shocked at her interpretation of our conversation, I let her know I had said no such thing. She informed me she was done with the rules, and she had already reported to her girlfriend that I'd told her to get out and had asked for a place to stay. I sat down on the arm of the couch, trying to process what was happening.

"Let's talk about this. Wait until your dad gets home," I pleaded with her.

A few more words passed between us that I can't recall, and I stood and walked closer to her, making one last attempt to convince her to stay until we could get her set up in her own place. But it was evident she had made up her mind. Emotionally, I was done fighting to save her from herself, and what I feared lay ahead for her. Finally, something inside me broke, and in a voice barely above a whisper, I said, "All right then, go." And as the words left my mouth, a guttural cry rose in me. "Go. Just go." My tone never elevated because there was no fight left in me to fight. I loved my daughter more than life itself, but I had no choice but to let her go.

She had barely walked out the door when my mom called, and wanting the comfort of my mother, I suppose, I answered the call. I tried to stay calm and hide what I was going through until she started in with her list of things she needed me to do. And I told her I couldn't and to find another sister to help her. I added that my husband and I were going through some stuff, and I needed time. She pressed me for more information, and I told her not to worry about it. She urged further, and for the first time ever, I raised my voice at my mother, venting all my panic and heartache on her.

"There ya have it. Are you happy? I screwed up. I've lost it all." I broke into a fit of uncontrollable tears. Then, after gathering my senses, I related to her what had happened.

Two hours after my daughter left home, I received a call from the paramedics that my daughter had overdosed and had been taken to the hospital. I grabbed my purse and my husband and raced for the car. I couldn't get to the hospital fast enough.

I couldn't understand what was happening. My daughter didn't do drugs. How could she have overdosed? I had done my best to be a checked-in parent, but I had no idea she had been smoking pot with her ex-boyfriend. This night, however, she took something someone else had purchased that was laced.

They showed my husband and me where she was being treated, and to stand there looking at your child, helpless and appearing in a vegetative state, is something I never want to experience again. We sat with her until the drugs were out of her system, and she opened her eyes. I thought she'd be grateful we had come, but instead, we were met with hostility. We took her home, and the next day she left on foot.

Days later, a friend at the time let me know that my daughter had told people that I had kicked her out and she had a horrible life at home. The knowledge shattered my heart. Why would she say such things? She had been given love, guidance, nurturance, and a safe haven. She had traveled the world and had all life's luxuries. Was that not enough?

When she returned home to gather the rest of her things, I was met with coldness and, again, aversion. I asked her to sit, and she did while I tried one more time to fix what was broken between us. As I spoke, silent tears streamed down my cheeks, and I told her I loved her, and this wasn't the way to go about securing her freedom. My pain was met with loathing, and her beautiful blue eyes turned dark with rage as she unleashed all the pain she had stored inside from her school years on me. I have never felt more hated in my life. It was as if I had stepped into the twilight zone. What had I done to make her hate me so? Yes, I had put rules in place. Isn't that what a good parent does? Where had I gone wrong?

As she spoke, I feared what would happen to her, out in the world on her own. She wasn't the most mature seventeen-year-old because she was my baby, and sheltered. And the fear that she hated me beyond repair gripped my heart. I realized I could not get through to her and told her to go ahead and get her stuff as my husband pulled into the driveway. I left her and went out to meet him to talk in private. I opened the passenger door to his truck, climbed in, and collapsed to my knees in a sobbing mess. I was overcome with emotions I didn't know how to process. Everything I had done was for nothing. My vision of success was raising healthy, happy kids and a future where we co-existed without toxicity. Instead, the happy family I had put all my efforts into was fractured, and I didn't know how to fix it.

I wondered if the drugs had hindered my daughter's capacity to feel and think clearly. It was like she had changed overnight. The anger and sharp tongue weren't the sweet, loving girl I knew.

My whole world had been shattered, and panic and grief seized every part of my being. I physically couldn't move. All I could do was lie on the couch and cry, and my six-month-old Australian Labradoodle would come and lick my tears. Dogs are amazing creatures, and I'm so thankful for my pup's love during that dark time. When exhaustion took over and I fell asleep, I'd make noises, and she'd come and nudge me with her cold nose to make sure I was all right.

I texted my daughter off and on, and each time I was met with anger. But I was determined to fight for her. I didn't seek to get her back home because that time had come to an end, but I wanted her in my life. I also wanted peace.

Within the first months of leaving home, she started experiencing severe panic attacks, and sleep paralysis became a nightly thing. I suggested she go to counseling and told her I'd pay. She agreed to go and went for a couple sessions before stopping. I realized then that I couldn't make her take care of herself or heal. I needed to stop trying to control the situation, and accept that what would be would be because, by this time, I was so stressed it was affecting my health. Migraines had become a daily thing, and the stress affected my hearing. The doctor set me up for hearing tests that came back normal; he ordered an MRI set for several months away.

I decided I would do what I knew best and go inward. I located a new counselor who specialized in trauma in hopes of gaining some piece of advice to heal the relationship between my daughter and me. My daughter's anger was projected at me, and not my husband or son.

My son, witnessing what we were going through, became angry at his sister. He still carried annoyance at her for the dynamics throughout their childhood. However, I noticed a change in him. He spent more time with us and appeared to enjoy being the only child in the house.

My first therapy appointment rolled around and, let me tell you, I was in for an awakening. Stepping into her office forced me to face major triggers before we even got started. She was a practicing Christian of some sort, and had gospel music playing and religious decor. Desperate for help, I didn't walk out when every part of me screamed, "run." I fixed my jaw and took a seat to wait. The gospel music made me question her professionalism. I wondered if she would try to shove her faith down my throat, remembering a previous experience with a counselor who had been more interested in speaking about Buddhism than helping me. I believe therapists should keep bias, opinions, and faith out of treatments. However, I was desperate for help, and when the therapist invited me in, she was warm and welcoming. Inside, I was still ticking, triggered by the music playing in the background. I'll clarify here and say that I sometimes listen to gospel music, so that wasn't what concerned me, but that she would try to force her belief system on me.

As I sat down, I noticed a decorative sign on her wall. The first word was *Christ*, and all that came after that blurred. By now my whole body was tense. First of all, I didn't like letting my guard down, and I didn't want to cry in front of other people. And how could I trust the counselor or her motives?

I continued seeing her for nine months and silently worked on my reactiveness to dealing with a religion-based person. Despite her knowledge of my childhood and the triggers I faced each time I came to her office, she continued to ask if I wanted to start with a prayer or take a moment of silence at the beginning of each session. And, in this respect, I felt disrespected because it coincided with my experience regarding the forcefulness of religion. She was aware that I preferred the moment of silence, so why keep pushing the matter? Again, I do pray, but on my own time, not with someone standing over me with a belt or when it's imposed on me. I politely declined her each time.

In the first few months of therapy I learned not to compare my parenting to my parents' and to trust that the adult me had the knowledge to parent better than they had. In releasing this vow I had made to myself to be anything but my parents, I allowed myself to trust in my abilities to be the mom my daughter needed. I released my need to fix the situation with my daughter, and did the only thing I knew how to do: be the mom I knew how to be. I removed my feelings from our interactions and applied love. I texted her a few times a week and told her I loved her and wished her a good day. Other times I texted her and asked her what time she worked, to which she usually replied. I showed up in the parking lot with her favorite latte or a care package of food. One of the first times, she came to the passenger window and I handed her what I had brought. Her eyes welled, and she said, "Why would you do this for me?"

"Because I'm your mom, and I love you."

It had been no different than what I had been doing for her all her life, but seeing her face, I recognized the guilt and shame she carried. She thanked me and walked inside. I made a conscious choice not to reinforce her guilt.

Although I shifted from needing to fix our situation to allowing it to naturally unfold, my devastation at having to meet her in her work parking lot to get a glimpse of her turned to anger when she opted out of seeing us for her birthday and the Christmas season.

Why had I become a mother in the first place? It was for sure the most thankless job, I told myself. I wallowed in my misery and, blinded by pain and anger, I developed the idea that she owed me—a perspective I'd loathed the most in my parents. The fact of the matter is, our children owe us nothing. Because we gave them life doesn't mean that, upon their birth, they enter a life of servitude. Our children are a gift and a blessing, entitled to their own free will and a life of their own. I had yet to understand how I still placed conditions on love. I would not gain this insight through therapy.

Against my better judgment, I reached out to my mother, craving maternal support. However, I received the same heartbreak and disappointment I usually did when dealing with her. She made the conversation about herself and the wrongs she believed her children had done to her. But of course when she made the statement "You reap what you sow," I disconnected from the conversation as rage reared inside me. I wanted to give her a piece of my mind. How dare she! I was tired of her back-handed remarks and beating around the bush regarding how she felt. I swallowed the pain and collected myself before speaking. I told her I hadn't done anything wrong to deserve God's wrath and that my leaving home the way I had had nothing to do with what was happening in my family. I went on to tell her that I regretted how I'd left home, but I didn't regret leaving. If I had to make a choice all over again, I would still have left.

My mother's attitude that day made me question my own. I had been carrying the belief for several months that my daughter had wronged me. Yes, she had made up lies about our family to gain other people's pity. It had broken our trust, and we had become leery of her. She had wounded the pride I felt at being what I deemed a good mom. I acknowledged I had fallen into a victim mentality, which served no purpose. But I didn't know how to shake myself free of it. My body ached night and day from the stress and suppressed anger. And as I had almost twenty years prior, I felt like I was going to have a mental breakdown. And that terrified me.

After Christmas that year, I drove white-knuckled in a blizzard to the therapist's office. The evening before, I sat in my office as my mind and body warned of a pending nervous breakdown. Minutes later, I received a call informing me of my uncle's death. Memories of my father's passing and the massive amounts of stress I endured to clean up his affairs brought fear and panic. *I can't do this again. I just can't.* But I had been given the task of informing my mother that her brother had passed. I made the call, and then while driving to my mother's work to pick her up, I considered my options and what I could do. I knew I wasn't mentally capable of taking on the burden of her pain or cleaning up another family member's affairs.

Later that evening, after long discussions and the frenzy of booking flights, I decided not to go with my mother and her sister. I knew I had to take care of myself, and I wasn't willing to cancel my two-hour therapist appointment the following morning, when they were scheduled to fly.

I made it to my therapist appointment and afterward, in my car, I paused to take a deep breath. I don't recollect anything the therapist said to elicit the change that took place next. But a sensation charged through my body, and it was as though I shook off the chains of bondage. I had craved liberation all my life, yet my conditioning had kept me prisoner. My soul cried for freedom. That day I told myself, no more! I would put myself first, step into my light, and heal myself once and for all.

I would come to understand the gift my daughter had presented to me the day she chose to claim her freedom. But first, I had to acquire the tools to release myself from my own oppression. These vital tools led me on the healing journey this book reveals.

One of my greatest desires in life has been to be the kind of mom I wanted to be. Not one shaped by societal conditioning or even one considered a "good" mom. Instead, I wanted to do it my way, shaped by how motherhood resonated with me. I wanted to be a diligent and devoted mother, the kind my kids understood had their backs and who they believed heard their voices. But I became over-engaged with my daughter because my fear of her suffering guided my daily interactions and decisions.

I sought to control her freedom to ward off harm, and in doing so I clipped her wings.

In discovering how to release my fears, step back, and allow my daughter to walk her own journey, I no longer rush in to fix her problems or anyone else's. I let my daughter learn from her experiences without fear of my disapproval. Instead, I receive her for all she is because love doesn't come with conditions. We can't mold people into what we think they should be. We must accept people for what they are and where they are in life. And we can't prevent our children from learning their life lessons.

During the year and a half that separated my daughter from us, I had no choice but to work on myself. I peeled back every layer of trauma blocked within me, and it was here, in the depths of great pain, that I came to understand that what I thought had been done to me was indeed done for me. I hadn't reaped what I sowed. I wasn't being punished because of past choices. I wasn't an unfit mother, nor had I failed. The love I held in my heart for my daughter didn't lead me astray, but it was the heartache, the deep-rooted pain, and the fear of stored memories that was the culprit. Only when rising above my pain did my vision clear enough to understand the gift I'd been granted.

23—THE HERO

"When we are afraid, we pull back from life. When we are in love, we open to all that life has to offer with passion, excitement, and acceptance. We need to learn to love ourselves first, in all our glory and our imperfections. If we cannot love ourselves, we cannot fully open to our ability to love others or our potential to create. Evolution and all hopes for a better world rest in the fearlessness and open-hearted vision of people who embrace life." ~ **John Lennon**

"I saw the angel in the marble and carved until I set him free."
~ **Michelangelo**

The persistent cry inside me has always been there—the song of my soul's desire to be free. I spent my life longing to be loved, and no amount of love in my life could permeate the hollowness inside me.

In my childhood, I cried out for a champion, but no one came to rescue me. I married a husband who became my lover, my soft place to fall, and my best friend, but all of that couldn't satisfy the grave emptiness and loneliness within me. No amount of love or support from loved ones or community could, until I realized no one was coming to save me. I had to save myself.

I became the hero in my story, and I have never found a more loyal ally than myself.

I had to chip through the superficial marble I had formed around myself to get to the thumping heart, scarred with years of trauma and heartache. I stood naked and exposed in my yearning to reveal the foundation and source of my pain.

I continued going to therapy until May of that year. I attended four hours that month, and during the sessions, we mucked around in my past. Unfortunately, as usual in my experience with therapy, the sessions left me with no understanding of how to deal with the residual pain afterward. Like a gaping wound without remedies to heal, the pain festered. The last session took me out for a week straight. Then, as I pulled myself back up, I found the resolution within me that would free me from the trauma once and for all.

Therapy wasn't working. So I left therapy for good. Treatments had cost me thousands, yet never provided the tools to release the anxiety and fear borne by the hurt and scared child existing inside of me. As much as therapy never offered a solution, neither did the anxiety medicines the doctors prescribed. The pills caused me to gain weight and had been a Band-Aid and nothing more.

After making the decision to leave therapy, I set out on a journey to find myself. I had never allowed myself to live for me. Instead, I'd spent my life caring for everyone else and suppressed my needs and what made me happy.

One day I decided to purchase my first gratitude journal. I stopped complaining about all the wrongs happening in my life and focused on the good.

My journey toward healing started with that simple decision. Gratitude. Yes, you read that correctly. Each morning I sat with a cup of coffee and my journal and wrote three things I was grateful for. Before I had become stressed, depleted, and angry at life, I would've considered myself a grateful person, but I had lost sight of all the good in my life.

A month later, an acquaintance led me to Louise Hay's book. This book sent me down a road of discovery no amount of therapy had ever given me. When I finished the book, I held it to my chest and wept. A switch had been turned on. Everything changed as I implemented the book's tools on self-love and uncovered layers of pain and fear. Her book would be the first stepping-stone toward discovering self-love, balance, and freedom from anxiety and past trauma. I wish I had known how easy it'd be to change a lifetime of fear, anxiety, and stress. I wish I had known I could've been free by reprogramming and calming my mind and loving myself first. To me, self-love had been pampering and treating myself to spa days to glam up my outer appearance. But self-love is so much more than that. We need to learn to love the very essence of who we are. We need to stop pushing ourselves away. Instead, we need to go to the shadow within us and work on the scars that have molded us. When we tune in to the whispering inside us, we will step into our personal power and find freedom and a love for life never experienced before.

For most of my life, a need to nurture and love inside of me was so overwhelming it felt like it would burst, and I poured this onto others when it was me that required it most. I yearned for a certain quality of love. A love that started within. Self-love.

I had been trained to run, hustle, and multitask to function in my childhood, which led to me running all my life, never slowing down or resting. I brushed my teeth while tidying the washroom. I finished one task or goal and quickly moved on to the next, never pausing to enjoy life because of this constant need to not fail and to show my worth. Some of these conditions are so hardwired within us that we don't see how they're cheating us of our quality of life. No wonder anxiety ran my life.

I learned to self-soothe at night. When I felt anxious, I would say, "It's okay, Naomi. I'm here. Everything will be all right. You are okay." I talked the little girl inside me off the ledge and pulled her into the safety of my motherly embrace. I learned to comfort my inner child the way I had mothered my own children. I treasured her. I told her she was beautiful and that I loved and accepted her. And, in time, she came to believe it.

Become the hero in your own life. Stop trying to prove yourself to others. You don't need anyone's approval. We've spent years unleashing abuse on our inner child. We constantly say, "If only you could be prettier, or slimmer, or more successful, then you would be enough. You would be lovable if you could just be all these things."

My challenge to you is, "Says who?" The one who abused you. The parent who didn't protect you. The parent you could never be enough for. The ex who berated and beat you. Why have you allowed their self-loathing emptied onto you to become your truth? That is their baggage. You aren't responsible for carrying it. So why are you letting yourself go down with them? It's time you board a flight of your choosing. One that's headed to a scenic destination called MY FUTURE.

My healing has allowed me to see my childhood for what it was. I do not downplay or ignore what happened, but I claimed my right to exist and be liberated from the hold it had on me. I felt all my pain. I uprooted every source of it and released it from my body, mind, and spirit. And each time I'm reactive, I go inward with the self-healing tools I've obtained. It's remarkable and inspiring how fast the emotions vanish and how much peace and tranquility have entered my life.

I broke down my walls and learned to ask for help when needed. To rest as required. To forgive me and others because liberation comes with letting go. I learned to believe in myself and become my own biggest supporter. I didn't need to be Superwoman. I didn't need to be anything but me. I took control of my own life. I freed my inner child and stepped into a future of my making. When I came to understand the external changes I also needed, my husband and I simplified our lives. We sold off our assets in one company holding us back and closed the doors, sold our home and all our possessions, and set out on an adventure to experience life with more freedom and joy. I let go of the need to control the outcome of my life. It is impossible to manage what is around the corner. All we have control of is the here and now. The present moment you now sit in holds power and is the key to receiving a life of your making. It's up to you to make the changes required.

Fly, My Darlings

"The two most important days in life are the day you are born, and the day you find out why." ~ **Mark Twain**

In a year or two from now, I will probably view some things in this book differently. As humans, we are constantly evolving, and I hope years from now that I'm a better version of myself because to remain in the same place you were five or ten years ago isn't the goal. We should be unfolding and raising our level of consciousness every day.

My journey isn't over, but I've collected powerful tools that have changed my life forever. Daily I work on myself. I found my freedom, and so can you.

We are brothers and sisters in this life together, trying to figure it all out. We can't change the past, but we can change our future. We have a responsibility to heal our own trauma and to do our part for future generations. Others cannot learn from us if we come from a place of malice and hate caused by unhealed pain. Blame is indeed a powerless act. It accomplishes nothing but keeps you stuck and hostage to yourself. We must step out of the blame game and into our lives. We can wallow in blaming our parents, colleagues, peers, the government, and the world for conditions they have imposed on us, and we will end up in the same discontented place for years to come. We want to hold our wrongdoers to the fire, make them own their wrongs, but what if that apology never comes? Do we allow our oppressors to also claim our future? No, that is our power. When we were children, we were incapable of protecting ourselves, but we can choose as adults. We can become our oppressors or break free of our self-imposed jails. This does not mean your feelings aren't valid.

There will be days when you don't feel like forgiving during the healing process, and that is okay. Take one day at a time, live in the here and now, and be gentle with yourself.

We need all our women, men, and children, and when we heal the fracture, we can come together to learn from each other. So, I say to all who are searching and have suffered, feel your pain, heal, and fly, my darlings! After all…we were all born to soar.

ABOUT THE AUTHOR

 Naomi is an author and entrepreneur residing in the beautiful Okanagan Valley, where hillside vineyards are the backdrop.

Her fascination with the human mind's power and becoming the observer in her own life have helped her heal from trauma.

She believes in the power of body, mind, and spirit and our ability to self-heal. In mothering the scared and wounded child trapped within, one can calm the mind and rid oneself of anxiety and fear.

Her passion is giving back, listening to the story behind the reactions, and helping others know they are heard and seen.

Sign up for my newsletter: naomicarr.me/newsletter

Made in the USA
Monee, IL
04 June 2024

59398999R00132